Indexed in

EGLI 1992

Indexed in

Idiom

Female Pastoral

Female Pastoral

Women Writers
Re-Visioning
the American South

Elizabeth Jane Harrison

The University of Tennessee Press
Knoxville

Copyright © 1991 by The University
of Tennessee Press / Knoxville.
All Rights Reserved.
Manufactured in the United States of America.
First Edition.

The paper in this book meets the minimum
requirements of the American National Standard
for Permanence of Paper for Printed Library Materials.
∞
The binding materials have been chosen
for strength and durability.

Library of Congress Cataloging in Publication Data

Harrison, Elizabeth Jane, 1960–
Female pastoral: women writers re-visioning the
American South / Elizabeth Jane Harrison.
     p.   cm.
Includes bibliographical references and index.
ISBN 0-87049-708-3 (cloth: alk. paper)
     1. Pastoral fiction, American—Southern States—History and
criticism. 2. Women and literature—Southern States—History—20th
century. 3. American fiction—Women authors—History and
criticism. 4. American fiction—20th century—History and criticism.
5. Southern States in literature. 6. Country life in literature. 7.
Landscape in literature. 8. Nature in literature. I. Title.
     PS261.H25   1991   90-28801
     813'.509321734—dc20   CIP

To Carolyn G. Heilbrun,
mentor and friend

Contents

Preface

My study of southern women writers began, as it seems to with many, as a personal quest. A product of the California suburbs, I had always envied those who knew more about their heritage, who had living records of their past through contact with relatives. My family's visits to my parents' hometown in rural Alabama were frequent enough to pique my curiosity. Why had my parents left? Why was my grandma so angry when my father came home? Why did my mother's six brothers and sisters host a family reunion every time we returned? These and other questions about my identity and heritage remained unspoken.

Oddly enough, I found myself teaching in Birmingham, Alabama, for a year before returning to graduate school. In the urban South, I began silently asking more questions. Was the sense of place less strong among city dwellers? What about class differences between urban and rural folk? Why was the South *still* such a patriarchal society? Was racial equality only a matter of civil rights, or was true understanding between black and white communities possible? Had the role of women really improved as the South became more industrialized?

Studying for my oral examinations, I re-formulated some of these questions as I surveyed American literature. Women characters created by women authors seemed to convey a sense of place deeper than and different from those imagined by male writers, who tended either to idealize or denigrate the "earth mother" figure. Comparing Willa Cather and Olë Rolvaag's characters, for instance, I found that the relationship of woman to the land was invariably energizing in the former and enervating in the latter.

"Local colorists," women authors, primarily, wrote with the same positive connections between women and the land as Cather did— Sarah Orne Jewett's Maine, Kate Chopin's Bayou, even Mary Murfree's southern mountains are just a few examples.

Southern women authors, especially, seemed to convey a strong sense of place. In the fiction of Flannery O'Connor, Eudora Welty, Zora Neale Hurston, and Margaret Walker, to name a few, I found that female identity was inevitably linked, not only to the southern society which nurtured—and often oppressed—their heroines, but also almost inexplicably to the land itself.[1]

I was particularly struck by the way in which some southern women authors re-imagined the South, revising such stereotypes as the plantation belle to show women, black and white, gaining autonomy by working on the land. From this observation came the realization that, far from "objectifying" women characters as part of the landscape, women writing in this way were creating a new form of celebratory "pastoral." Instead of lamenting the loss of a rural world through nostalgia, these women authors were envisioning new worlds, different kinds of communities. The connection of women to the land and to nature somehow enabled a new vision.

The six authors I have chosen for this study are not necessarily representative of a "genre" of "female pastoral," although I did attempt to identify elements of female autonomy and revisionary communities in each. One important prerequisite for the female pastoral vision, I discovered, was an abandonment of what Carolyn Heilbrun calls the "courtship plot."[2] Romance is no longer the main focus of fiction in this new tradition; instead the reactive heroine becomes active hero—she begins her own quest.

Ellen Glasgow, whose rural novels I consider in chapter 1, creates a memorable female hero in *Barren Ground*. Dorinda Oakley's triumph over the land enables her to assert a new identity for herself outside the prescribed roles of wife and mother. In her later pastoral, *Vein of Iron*, Glasgow explores the idea of community in returning the character, Ada, and her family to their rural homeland. Margaret Mitchell's *Gone with the Wind*, the subject of chapter 2, is perhaps ironically both a celebration of female power and a perpetuation of patriarchal southern plantation myth. Nonetheless, like Glasgow, Mitchell experiments with gender roles and revises interactions among community members.

My selection of Willa Cather's last novel, *Sapphira and the Slave Girl*, for chapter 3, may seem an odd inclusion to some, since most of Cather's fiction centers on the midwestern landscape. But, as an anti-plantation romance, it provides an effective countertext to *Gone with the Wind* in exposing a black woman as sexual victim of her white mistress's drive for power. In this novel, female autonomy is threatened by the male tendency to objectify woman through "naturalizing" her—identifying her as symbolic of landscape rather than energized by it. Cather's imagery of an interracial female community offers a partial healing for the wounds of slavery.

Arnow's *The Dollmaker* is the focus of chapter 4. Protagonist Gertie's exile from her rural homeland both enables her to realize autonomy and artistic identity and shows the devastating effects on female autonomy resulting from loss of place. The transitory, but vital, alliance of women that emerges in the alley of the Neveleses' housing project presents another version of female community. In chapter 5, my discussion of Alice Walker's *The Color Purple* also explores the connection between female creativity and nature. The novel exposes the double burdens of sexism and racism that black women characters must overcome in the rural South. At the end of the novel, Walker imagines a reconciliation between the men and women of her farm community. Sherley Williams, who like Cather is not usually associated with the South, nonetheless explores her southern heritage in her poetry and fiction. Her novel *Dessa Rose*, the focus of chapter 6, envisions an egalitarian interracial community through the use of a historical antebellum setting. The understanding between Dessa and Rufel, a black woman and a white woman, reconfirms the possibility of friendship that crosses boundaries of race and status.

Studying these novels has helped me to answer some questions about my own southern heritage. The homesickness of Harriette Arnow's Gertie Nevels for her rural Kentucky home makes me realize why my grandparents were so reluctant to leave Alabama even for short visits to the West and perhaps explains why my grandmother felt my father had abandoned her. Dorinda Oakley's desire—and need—to own and work on the land in *Barren Ground* demonstrates how closely female identity is tied to meaningful labor. After years of running a roadside motel, my grandmother must have felt a loss of "self" once the new interstate highway forced her and my grandfather to close the business. The interracial female friendship that develops in Cather's *Sapphira and the Slave Girl* and Williams's *Dessa Rose* gives me hope that black and white women might move beyond establishing legal and social equality to become true friends. This friendship may have to be realized in fiction, however, before it can become an actuality.

New visions—new plots—created by southern women writers thus might call us to the future as well as help us understand our past. My exploration of a female pastoral tradition might, I hope, provide one starting point for such a quest.

Acknowledgments

Before reading any book I always turn to the preface and acknowledgements because there, I realize, lies the true record of its creation. My book is no exception. I am grateful to many friends and colleagues who helped directly and indirectly with the progress of my manuscript from nascent dissertation prospectus to its present form.

First, I wish to acknowledge my advisor, Professor Carolyn G. Heilbrun, to whom I dedicate this book. Without her generosity, encouragement, and prompt and insightful readings, I would have never completed it. Two dissertation groups at Columbia University also helped me revise and focus my argument. In particular, I want to thank Suvendi Perera, who has carefully read every chapter, as well as Susan Heath and Lisa Gitelman. Laura Henigman and Priscilla Wald, who served on my dissertation defense, gave additional helpful suggestions.

Lillian Morrison has been an indispensable editor, critic, and friend. Many other friends have encouraged me along the way— Danny Miller read and gave suggestions on *The Dollmaker* chapter; Anne Jones read and discussed with me the *Gone with the Wind* chapter. I am grateful to the members of the English Department at West Virginia State College who helped revive my interest in revising my dissertation.

More recently, my colleagues at Berea College have helped me reshape the introduction. I would like to thank especially Libby Jones, Jane Olmsted, Bill Schafer, Mary Jo Thomas, and Barbara Wade.

I want to acknowledge permissions from the following publishers:

Harcourt Brace Jovanovich for permission to quote from *The Color Purple* by Alice Walker, copyright 1982.

Russell and Volkening as agents of the author for permission to quote from *The Dollmaker* by Harriette Arnow, copyright 1954 by Harriette Arnow, renewed in 1982 by the author.

Alfred A. Knopf, Inc., for permission to quote from *Sapphira and the Slave Girl* by Willa Cather, copyright 1940.

William Morrow and Company for permission to quote from *Dessa Rose* by Sherley Williams, copyright 1986.

A different version of chapter 1 appeared as "Ellen Glasgow's Revision of the Southern Pastoral" in *South Atlantic Review* 55 (May 1990): 47–70.

Finally, and most of all, I wish to thank my family: my parents, Don and Laura Harrison, and my siblings, Donna and David Marks, Doug Harrison, and Jama Greene. Their support and encouragement has been immeasurable.

Female Pastoral

Introduction: Revising the Male Pastoral Tradition

> Re-vision—the act of looking back, of seeing with fresh eyes, of entering an old text from a new critical direction—is for women more than a chapter in cultural history: it is an act of survival. Until we can understand the assumptions in which we are drenched we cannot know ourselves. And this drive to self-knowledge, for women, is more than a search for identity: it is part of our refusal of the self destructiveness of male-dominated society.
>
> —Adrienne Rich

> That the metaphorical experience of the land-as-woman appears now to have only dangerous consequences does not, I hope, mean we have lost our capacity to create adaptive symbols for ourselves, but only that the one we had has now run its course. . . . The very fact that the archetypal polarities, masculine and feminine, are now undergoing radical alterations in the ways they are imaged and perceived suggests that, insofar as the pastoral metaphor partakes of this polarity, it too may be undergoing changes that will, in the end, prove adaptive and survival-oriented. It is even possible that the choice is already ours . . . .
>
> —Annette Kolodny

The word "pastoral" conjures up vague and contradictory associations, particularly as a literary term. To many, the image of shepherds in a bucolic landscape comes to mind, evoking the Renaissance concept of Arcadia, that Edenic green world where the evils of the court could be escaped however temporarily. In modern literature, "pastoral" is used more loosely to suggest any literary work, poem or prose, that idealizes the rural world.[1]

Many critics of American literature have been fascinated by the concept of America as a New World Eden. Richard Chase, Henry Nash Smith, Leslie Fielder, Leo Marx, and others have documented such a "pastoral" tendency beginning with James Fenimore Cooper's Leatherstocking tales. Focusing particularly on novels that emphasize the settlement and conquering of the frontier, these literary scholars, from 1950 on, have canonized a specific pastoral tradition. In the 1970s, feminist scholars began to question this critical approach. Annette Kolodny and Nina Baym observed that women characters, especially, held no place in the conquest of the virgin landscape. Kolodny wrote two studies of the archetype of the American landscape. Her first, *The Lay of the Land* (1975), redefines the American pastoral as "the yearning to know and respond to the landscape as feminine" (8); and her second, *The Land Before Her: Fantasy and Experience of the American Frontiers, 1630–1860* (1980), explores how women pioneers in the nineteenth century responded to the landscape quite differently than men through diaries and letters.

My study begins where Kolodny's ends. It explores twentieth-century women writers' responses to landscape in order to determine whether they are finally able to overcome the pervasive masculine "pastoral impulse" and establish an alternative tradition of their own. I focus on the South, rather than the westward pioneer movement as Kolodny does, because it is where the concept of virginal land most firmly took hold. Critic Lewis Simpson believes that the South envisioned itself as an *improved* paradise or cultivated garden in order to expiate its guilt over chattel slavery. This purpose contrasts sharply, he claims, with the New England vision of the City on a Hill, which was formed in order to establish a religious covenant rather than legitimize an economic and historical oppression (2). Whatever the origin of the garden archetype, it served the southern white patriarchy—including its male authors—for over two hundred years as an effective metaphor of ownership of both land and labor.

By the early nineteenth century, as W. J. Cash and others have documented, a pastoral tradition in southern literature had been established as a means of perpetuating a myth of aristocratic origins and defending the slave system.[2] The first iteration of the male pastoral impulse in the South was as antebellum romance. William Gilmore Simms, often considered the southern counterpart of James Fenimore Cooper, wrote in this tradition. Like Cooper, Simms imagined the white woman as a civilizing, moral influence, while simultaneously depicting her "naturalized" beauty. Simms's 1835 novel, *The Yemassee*, depicts the settlement of the aristocratic English cavalier in the American South. An English nobleman, Gabriel Harrison, arrives in the colony of South Carolina to save it from attack by Indian savages. The South is imagined as a kind of new Eden, an unspoiled garden where the aristocratic society could flourish. White southern womanhood represents this virgin land, of course, and by protecting her, the cavalier upholds his patriarchal ideals and defends his homeland from defilement by intruders.

John Pendleton Kennedy's *Swallow Barn* (1832), considered by many as the first true plantation novel, presents the favorable reaction of a northern visitor to the genteel society he encounters on his journey through the South. Following Kennedy, other writers imitated the traveler's report format in order to depict and defend their slaveholding society.[3]

After the Civil War, a second but closely related kind of male pastoral emerged. The plantation or Lost Cause school of fiction invoked the so-called "lost" aristocratic society. Late nineteenth-century pastorals reiterated a common theme—reconciliation between the South and North, accomplished through using the white woman as an instrument of the plot. Typically, the pristine plantation daughter was married to a northern soldier or gentleman to symbolize the healing of the Union. The contented "darky" narrator, another salient feature of the pastoral plot, reinforced the continuance of a pastoral society in which both white women and blacks were viewed as property. Thomas Nelson Page's *In Ole Virginia* (1887), a collection of stories about antebellum plantation life, epitomizes this version of male pastoral. Black narrators fiercely loyal to their old masters are featured in each tale. In "Meh Lady," former slave narrator Billy unites his plantation mistress with a colonel in the Union army, a plot device which, like the agreeable northern traveler in antebellum pastorals, figuratively reasserts the pastoral myth.[4]

Postbellum pastorals thus actually furthered the association of the white southern lady with the land of the South itself. But it is important *not* to consider the representation of white southern womanhood in isolation. In discussing African-American writers of the nineteenth century, Hazel Carby points out that, in "order to perceive the cultural effectivity of ideologies of black female sexuality, it is necessary to consider the determining force of ideologies of white female sexuality: stereotypes only appear to exist in isolation while actually depending on a nexus of figurations which can be explained only in relation to each other" (*Reconstructing Womanhood* 20).

The aristocratic southern lady's association with culture and refinement—her embodiment of the southern garden—thus depended upon a counterimage, the black or poor white woman. While the genteel lady ideologically represented purity, her dark counterpart was objectified as debased sexual desire. Each of these stereotypes had its obverse image, however. Along with her sexual availability and "breeder" status, the black woman also became the beloved "mammy" figure, the archetypal earth mother who nurtured white and black protagonists alike. The white lady symbolized a "fallen" Eve in a postlapsarian garden. According to Kathryn Lee Seidel, two versions of the plantation romance developed: one holding northerners and blacks accountable for the evil invasion of the southern garden, and the other blaming the white woman herself, who in this case becomes a seductress figure (127–34).

As the century waned, the male pastoral became more a hysterical defense of the white patriarchy than a nostalgic idealization of a genteel society. The extreme racism in Thomas Dixon's fiction expresses an increasing fear of the potential empowerment of the oppressed, and the popularity of this genre coincided with the rise of Jim Crow.[5] Initially conceived as a conservative genre before the Civil War, postbellum southern pastorals became both a reflection of the dominant mood of the culture and a means of shaping and reinforcing racist and misogynist views.

Although at the turn of the century authors like George Washington Cable and Charles Chesnutt began to criticize and challenge this genre, the myth of the southern garden persisted.[6] The southern "renaissance" that occurred after World War I marks a third version of the southern male pastoral; the imagery of the despoiled southern garden remains constant. Well-respected analysts like Richard King and Lewis Simpson canonize this pastoral as the eminent form of the period while ignoring fiction that works against it.[7]

But the southern male pastoral between the world wars begins to show the influence of the rising social upheaval. No longer could the garden archetype function as a displacement of sectional conflict. Now the threat to property was internal. White patriarchy had begun to lose economic and political power through such movements as women's suffrage, urbanization, and finally civil rights.[8] Literature reflects fear of these social changes in the negative portrayal of white and black women. In volume 1 of *No Man's Land: The Place of the Woman Writer in the Twentieth Century*, Sandra Gilbert and Susan Gubar reveal how tensions between the sexes were a major component of the modernist period in literature (21). This sexual battle, in addition to racial unrest, is a prevalent though unacknowledged feature of southern renaissance fiction.

One modern version of southern pastoral that reveals sexual and racial tension is agrarian Allen Tate's *The Fathers* (1939), a novel which ostensibly explores the passing of the antebellum order in the conflict between Major Buchan and his son-in-law, George Posey. But Tate's overt historical plot disguises a text supporting oppression. Another important battle in the novel occurs between George and his wife Susan. She literally arranges for the rape of her young sister-in-law, Jane, by a mulatto slave in order to remove her from the patriarchal order. Now "ruined," the young girl is sent to a convent rather than marrying. Susan's power play proves too much for her, though: she goes quietly mad at the end of the novel. George's compassion for Yellow Jim, the mulatto slave who attacked his sister-in-law, and, more significantly, his own half-brother, is undercut by his inability to challenge or change the system he inherits. He may represent a new order, but it resembles more than differs from the previous one. Tate's novel imagines and then suppresses different power relationships: the representation of Susan and Yellow Jim shows how the southern myth favors stereotypes over individual character development.[9]

Just as in the two earlier versions of southern male pastoral, in the modern period, blacks and white women were literally and metaphorically considered "property." Since women were connected symbolically with land ownership, the loss of property might be represented in fiction as rape. The rape of the white woman in such twentieth-century versions of the southern male pastoral as *The Fathers* thus can be seen as a violation of property. And the proliferation of historical novels like *The Fathers* suggests that preoccupation with the past, or nostalgia for an "old order," was actually a reaction to contemporary changes in the political and social status of white women and blacks.

Not all fictional representations of women emphasized their violation or corruption, though. William Faulkner and a few other male authors of the southern renaissance recast the earth mother stereotype with their portrayals of poor white and black women.

Lena Grove in Faulkner's *Light in August* (1932) typifies a new version of southern womanhood. The poor white, rural woman replaces her aristocratic counterpart as redeemer. Separated by class, she does not threaten patriarchal control. Lena becomes the fecund progenitor of a new generation of white southerners—a means by which the sins of the past (i.e., slavery and miscegenation) can be forgotten. *Light in August* is often considered by Faulkner critics as "pastoral" in the classical sense: Lena is seen as a Keatsian "harvest girl," and her "otherness" is equated with a serene natural force. She becomes the unifying symbol of the novel. According to André Bleikasten, "Lena is light, as 'Helen was light,' and she is also, according to one of the oldest metaphors of womanhood, an urn, a body-vessel destined to receive man's seed" (138). Woman may be idealized, but she is still objectified in this version of pastoral.

Black women characters are also naturalized in the modern male pastoral. Faulkner's Dilsey in *The Sound and the Fury* (1929) functions much like Lena as a life force, and, while it is Caddy who is specifically associated with nature or trees, as postbellum "mammy" Dilsey assumes the mythic role of earth mother in this novel. Even more than white women characters, black women are associated with property ownership, and they are also victimized by rape, though "rape" is never the term used. Despite the sympathy of Mr. Compson, Nancy's terror in Faulkner's "That Evening Sun" is exaggerated to the point of ridicule; her husband's abuse (she knows he will return to beat or kill her) is undercut by the Compson children's "innocent" antics and Dilsey's "sensible" advice. In contrast to the faithful servant Dilsey, Nancy is presented as a hopelessly superstitious "nigger." Portrayed either as whore or nurturer, the twentieth-century black woman character still conforms to nineteenth-century stereotypes.

Although black authors Jean Toomer and James Weldon Johnson revived southern rural fiction with their depiction of the "folk" during this period, neither challenged the pastoral plot of domination or questioned the archetype of black woman as earth mother. Toomer's *Cane* (1923), sometimes considered black pastoral,[10] expresses more ambivalence about the possibility of change

in the rural world, and although it celebrates black women's creativity, it also stereotypes their sexuality. After Toomer, few male
African-American novelists reevaluated the southern landscape.
Instead, critics favored novels of escape from the South like Richard Wright's *Black Boy* (1945) and Ralph Ellison's *Invisible Man*
(1952). Both white and black male authors continued the objectification of women characters through the earth mother stereotype.

For twentieth-century women writers, nonetheless, all these
representations of female character are problematic. None allows
for full psychological development of a woman protagonist. As
Sandra Gilbert and Susan Gubar have demonstrated, women in
literature and art are traditionally viewed as object, not active
subject, so the creative process is doubly difficult for a woman
writer.[11] She cannot envision either herself or her characters as
autonomous without changing archetypal patterns. Nina Baym
illustrates the problem for women authors confronting the male
"pastoral impulse":

> I have said that women are not likely to cast themselves as
> antagonists in a man's story; they are even less likely, I suggest, to
> cast themselves as virgin land. The lack of fit between their own
> experience and the fictional role assigned to them is even greater
> in the second instance than in the first. If women portray
> themselves as brides or mothers it will not be in terms of the
> mythic landscape. If a woman puts a female construction on
> nature. . . she is likely to write of it as more active, or to stress its
> destruction or violation. . . . When the woman writer creates a story
> that conforms to the expected myth, it is not recognized for what it
> is because of a superfluous sexual specialization in the myth as it is
> entertained in the critics' minds. . . . But if she does not conform
> to the myth, she is understood to be writing minor or trivial
> literature. (75–76)

Like Baym, I argue that women writers had to create a new
landscape imagery, not only to enable their female protagonists to

emerge beyond symbolic representation as virginal or despoiled land, but also to create a legitimate artistic tradition for themselves. Since the only way to write within the existing archetypal structure is to adopt a male voice, the process of creating an alternative female pastoral tradition is thus crucial for southern women writers.

In 1913 Willa Cather's *O Pioneers!* launched what I define as the first successful attempt to change the relationship between women and landscape. Cather's protagonist, Alexandra Bergson, clearly establishes her autonomy through an empowering bond with nature. She draws identity *from* the land rather than becoming symbolic *of* it. In the same year, southern author Ellen Glasgow began her critique of the southern patriarchy with her novel *Virginia*, which begins to question the male view of woman as flower of his archetypal garden.

But for black women novelists, the persistent stereotype of the debased black woman made a challenge to the male pastoral plot more difficult. As the Schomburg Library's recent reissuing of lost nineteenth-century novels by black women reveals, African-American women writers first had to overcome the stigma of racial inferiority before they could imagine an empowering relationship between women characters and the land. "Land" for them was associated with slave labor, and female slaves, particularly, had been featured in slave narratives as victims of sexual assault by white slave owners. Frances Foster explains in an introduction to Francis Harper's 1893 novel, *Iola Leroy,* that after the Civil War, narratives by black writers were no longer acclaimed solely on the basis of their abolitionist subject matter, and by the 1890s, standards for publishing black fiction had become quite stringent (xxvii–xxix). African-American women authors first had to write against slave-narrative conventions expected by a white audience before they could establish an alternative tradition of their own. Deborah McDowell calls turn-of-the-century novels by black women "public" narratives in the sense that they address "a public reader-

ship, or one outside the black cultural community," and contrasts
them to contemporary African-American fiction like Alice Walker's
The Color Purple which imply a "private" readership (1987, 282).

Comparing contemporary texts by black and white women
might illustrate how black women authors were concerned with a
public audience until a later date. Kate Chopin's *The Awakening*
and Pauline Hopkins's *Contending Forces* were both published in
1899, and both concern Creole society. Chopin's novel focuses on
the self-realization of the female protagonist, Edna, who, although
she cannot complete her act of rebellion, refuses to sacrifice her
life and vocation for her family. Hopkins, on the contrary, constructs a plot around the question of racial identity and heritage.
She states in her preface that her purpose is to "raise the stigma of
degradation from my race" (13).

Like the earlier *Iola Leroy*, Hopkins's *Contending Forces* favors
public over private narrative. Sappho's public identity matters
more than what she wants to be. Heritage determines character
and behavior. Not until over twenty years later with the Harlem
Renaissance novels of Nella Larsen and Jessie Fauset do African-
American women novelists depict a female quest for self-fulfill-
ment like Edna Pontellier's. One reason, then, for the time lag
between the development of the white and black female pastoral
might be different audience expectations and the necessity for
African-American authors to overcome both racist and sexist
stereotypes.

Nonetheless, beginning with Zora Neale Hurston's *Their Eyes
Were Watching God* in 1937, black women writers, like their white
southern counterparts, begin to reexamine the pastoral world. I
discuss these white and black female versions of the southern
pastoral chronologically, not so much to show a direct relationship
among them, as to explore ways in which their differences express
an evolving vision of a new southern society.

This alternative female pastoral, like its corresponding male
genre, contains specific elements. First, landscape itself figures

prominently in the text, but instead of representing southern womanhood it is "re-visioned" as an enabling force for the woman protagonist. Her interaction with land changes from passive association to active cultivation or identification. For black women authors in this new tradition, nature is an overriding force that must be respected rather than overcome or tamed as it is in the white version.[12] For both black and white authors the female pastoral becomes, unlike the male tradition, a liberating, visionary genre rather than a reactionary or critical one.

As Judith Weissman explains in the introduction to her study *Half Savage and Hardy and Free: Women and Rural Radicalism in the Nineteenth-Century Novel,* such a revision of the male pastoral world does not necessarily entail utopianism. Rather, such novels about female rural experience might offer

> a vision of political radicalism that is tied to an agricultural
> economy, and to forms of labor that can evade the oppressive and
> unjust structures of capitalism. They do not offer freedom from
> labor and action, a life of pure leisure and pleasure. They demand
> action that we stand up for a threatened and valuable economic
> system which is a genuine alternative to both the capitalism of
> industry and the capitalism of the kind of farming which reduces
> laborers to degraded paupers.(8)

The twentieth-century American novels I examine participate in this same kind of quest. "Pastoral" may be a misleading term since it is most often used to designate a gentried or leisure class. The female pastoral I define envisions new class relationships and stresses not individual but cooperative action.

Changing the representation of landscape as female allows for changes in the pastoral plot as well. No longer must it be concerned with domination and the inscription of a patriarchal order. By freeing her protagonist from a narrow association with the southern garden, the southern woman author not only can define a new female hero—woman as active agent—but also begin to imagine a new society, one in which communal values replace

hierarchical ones. Initially, the communities imagined in novels
about female heroes might be comprised primarily of women.
Nina Auerbach defines these women's communities as "a rebuke
to the conventional ideal of a solitary woman living for and
through men, attaining citizenship in the community of adult-
hood through masculine approval alone" (5). Women's communities allow the female protagonist to develop autonomy and authority outside the larger, patriarchal society.

Eventually, however, by reshaping interactions among men
and women, these authors imagine egalitarian societies similar to
what sociologist Robert Bellah calls "communities of memory." In
such communities, instead of an emphasis on self-reliance, a *positive*
sense of tradition and history enables community members to
retell the community's "story, its constitutive narrative," and "offer
examples of the men and women who have embodied and exemplified the meaning of the community" (153). Unlike the southern agrarians' rural vision of the 1930s, which envisioned a society
of Jeffersonian yeomen, in communities of memory the past enables a coherent vision of the future. It does not merely provide a
blueprint of the status quo. The rural worlds pictured by female
pastoral begin with Weissman's and Auerbach's ideas about female
autonomy and move toward Bellah's vision of cooperative community.

The pastorals I have chosen for this study do not epitomize a
new genre (two in fact depart from land cultivation), but they do
share a vision of rural female autonomy from Ellen Glasgow's
revised plantation romances to Sherley Williams's recent historical
novel about escaped slaves who take refuge on a white woman's
plantation. Although the African-American pastoral may originate
from a different literary tradition, the slave narrative, which favors
escape from the South, I believe that the black female pastoral has
much in common with a corresponding white female form.

Both work against prevailing literary models, the plantation
romance and the concomitant "local color" fiction which stereo-

typed poor farmers as pathetic, stupid, or ridiculous characters.[13] Women authors subvert these two genres by rescuing the female protagonist from her role as plantation mistress or mammy in anti-plantation romances or, alternately, by re-imagining the poor tenant farmer as an independent landowner. The pastorals I discuss may be roughly categorized in these two groups: Margaret Mitchell, Willa Cather, and Sherley Williams revise the plantation model while Ellen Glasgow, Harriette Arnow, and Alice Walker rework the "poor white" or "folk" tradition.

In the six novels I examine, both black and white versions of the southern garden challenge a reductive view of women characters, and both use land or nature as a means of liberation from an oppressive society. By disassociating the woman protagonist from her representation *as* landscape, the female pastoral first allows her to develop autonomy. She becomes aware of herself as a sexual *being* rather than as object. No longer the "property" of her husband or of the land tenancy system (in which black and white farmers were essentially chattel), the woman protagonist overcomes exploitation—and in the female pastoral the rape scene so central to the male southern pastoral is significantly altered.

Nature becomes an enabling force or "character" in the plot through which the protagonist can derive strength and fulfill passion. Dorinda Oakley in Ellen Glasgow's *Barren Ground* defines a new role for herself in society as farmer and landowner. She transfers her passion for a lover who jilted her to a passion for her work on the land. Scarlett O'Hara's return to Tara at the end of *Gone with the Wind* reflects the same tendency, not to substitute work for sexual passion, but to recognize meaningful labor as a related *kind* of sexuality that is equally fulfilling. Celie's cottage industry of creating folkspants in Alice Walker's *The Color Purple* results not only from Shug's encouragement but from her own developing awareness of herself as an individual empowered by her connection to nature.

This liberation from objectification also enables the protago-

nist to challenge her appointed role as wife and childbearer. The
female pastoral moves beyond the romantic plot. New kinds of
relationships between men and women are imagined. In *Barren
Ground,* Dorinda and Nathan marry for expediency rather than
love; then, they develop a friendship through their shared love for
the land. Likewise in *Gone with the Wind* Scarlett and Will Benteen,
the poor white she appoints as Tara's overseer, develop a relationship of mutual respect and affection out of their devotion to the
plantation. In Williams's *Dessa Rose,* Dessa and Nathan can freely
express their love for each other as friends without the romantic
conventions of sexual passion or marriage.

Different relationships among women are also envisioned. No
longer divided from one another as "property" of a patriarchal
system, they are free to become friends without competition for
male attention. Glasgow's *The Miller of Old Church* reveals this connection as Molly reaches out to comfort the heartbroken Blossom,
and *Gone with the Wind* shows female friendship through Scarlett
and Melanie. It is harder for women to form friendships across
class and race barriers, nonetheless. The tentative women's community that develops at Merry Hill in Harriette Arnow's *The Dollmaker* is threatened by conflicting alliances to family and society as
is the interracial bonding among Nancy, Rachel, and Till at the
end of Cather's *Sapphira and the Slave Girl.* White women cannot
easily break away from privileges afforded them by the southern
patriarchy—as Eleanor Jane in *The Color Purple* and Rufel in *Dessa
Rose* demonstrate.

Finally, the female pastoral moves toward a new definition of
rural community, not framed on the eighteenth-century Jeffersonian model of the independent yeoman but more akin to
Bellah's definition of communities of memory. The conclusions of
Ellen Glasgow's later pastorals, particularly *Vein of Iron,* and Alice
Walker's *The Color Purple* envision farm communities where shared
labor eliminates class, race, and gender hierarchy.

Despite difficulties in overcoming the barriers to sex and race equality, female friendship and cooperative communities become an important part of the new southern garden for these women authors. Their explorations of ways of achieving female autonomy and changing interactions among characters of different class, race, and gender depend upon the invocation of land not as "property" but as an empowering life source. This alternative pastoral questions the motivations of a society that ignores exploitation of others for the sake of land ownership. Respect for the land enables respect for all human life. The next six chapters trace these authors' attempts to create such a pastoral vision.

1. Ellen Glasgow's Evolution of the Southern Pastoral: From *The Battle-Ground* to *Vein of Iron*

While the Soil endured, while the seasons bloomed
and dropped, while the ancient, beneficent ritual sowing
and reaping moved in the fields, she knew that she could
never despair of contentment.

—*Barren Ground*

Before creating a female agrarian hero in her 1925 novel, *Barren Ground*, Ellen Glasgow had to evolve a new tradition of pastoral fiction from the typical nineteenth-century plantation romance, for unlike her midwestern contemporary, Willa Cather, she did not leave her native South to establish an artistic home in a place free from the male "pastoral impulse." Often credited as the author who brought realism "across the Potomac," Glasgow was not only critical of the chivalric code in novels such as *Virginia* (1913), but also, I believe, began early in her career to develop an alternate version of the naturalistic novel in order to reshape the southern pastoral, a form identified earlier as a genre that inscribes a racist patriarchal order.[1]

The author's early fiction, in fact, has often been misconstrued as social chronicle rather than aesthetic innovation. While her concerns for rural reform and the effete aristocracy are important, few critics consider the connection between her depiction of the rural world and her creation of a new kind of pastoral.[2] Glasgow's early pastorals represent partly successful attempts to refashion the mythic southern garden. Her rejection of the plantation tradition begins in *The Battle-Ground* (1902), her fourth novel, where she changes the focus of the narrative from the defeated aristocracy to a new yeoman class of farmers. While she writes this novel "with the spirit of romance," as befitting a Civil War story (*A Certain Measure* 24), she also subtly injects an ironic point of view toward some of the more "stock" characters like Major Lightfoot and Betty's sister, Virginia. Pinetop, her first realistic portrait of a poor white character, also appears in this novel.[3]

With *The Battle-Ground* and continuing with *The Deliverance* (1904) and *The Miller of Old Church* (1911), the two other novels of her early period that employ a rural setting, the author sets up a dichotomy between the ordered antebellum world and the emerging yet latent community of independent farmers. The description of the plantation, a convention in pastoral romances, becomes a device to criticize the old order. The character's view of nature, represented in the following passage where Betty's father, Mr. Ambler, surveys his land, not only reflects his attitude toward this oppressive order but indicates the narrator's critical stance:

> The master of Uplands was standing upon his portico behind the Doric columns, looking complacently over the fat lands upon which his fathers had sown and harvested for generations. . . . his eyes wandered leisurely across the blue green strip of grass-land to the tawny wheat field, where the slaves were singing as they swung their cradles. The day was fine, and the outlying meadows seemed to reflect his gaze with a smile as beneficent as his own. He had cast his bread upon the soil, and it had returned to him threefold.
>
> As he stood there, a small, yet imposing figure, in his white duck suit, holding his broad slouch hat in his hand, he presented something of the genial aspect of the country—as if the light that touched the pleasant hills and valleys was aglow in his clear brown eyes and comely features. Even the smooth white hand in which he held his hat and riding whip had about it a certain plump kindli-ness which would best become a careless gesture of concession. And, after all, he looked but what he was—a bald and generous gentleman, whose heart was as open as his wine cellar. (45)

The description here is intentionally ironic. The contrast between what "seems" to be with the actuality of the menace of war and the complete annihilation of the society in which Mr. Ambler lives is rendered through the conditional tense and the subtle misuse of metaphor. Mr. Ambler casts his bread upon the ground, not the waters as in the Biblical verse, and for all his "kindliness" and "generous" nature, he is nonetheless the owner of an oppressive institution. His "smooth white hand" depends upon other hands that use the whip *without* concession in order to cultivate his "tawny wheat field." The master of Uplands is only speciously in harmony with nature here. Later, the reader discovers the consequences of his disregard for the exploitation of others.

The Deliverance and *The Miller of Old Church* use the device of the approaching visitor to establish the distance between the characters' and narrator's attitudes. Unlike Thomas Nelson Page, however, Glasgow makes the intruding urban skeptic a southerner, not a northerner, thus complicating the city versus country schematic. As Mr. Carraway arrives at the Blake plantation in the opening scene of *The Deliverance*, we see the narrator's equivocating viewpoint, at once condemning and identifying with Carraway's disillusionment:

> For more than two hundred years Blake Hall had stood as the one great house in the county—a manifestation in brick and mortar of the hereditary greatness of the Blakes. To Carraway, impersonal as his interest was, the acknowledgment brought a sudden vague resentment, and for an instant he bit his lip and hung irresolute, as if more than half-inclined to retrace his steps. (15)

Beneath the surface anxiety about the passing order of the aristocracy, the narrator gently mocks Carraway's "impersonal" interest in the shift of ownership, for after all, Fletcher's takeover marks an overturning of the whole social fabric and threatens Carraway's status as much as it destroys the Blakes.

In *The Miller of Old Church* an even more misunderstanding intruder appears. Jonathan Gay returns to his rural homeland after spending several years away at school and abroad. The narrator gives us his initial, almost fearful reaction to the pastoral scene before him:

> . . . the character of the country underwent so sudden a
> transformation that it looked as if man, having contended here
> unsuccessfully with Nature, had signed an ignominious truce
> beneath the crumbling gate-posts of the turnpike. Passing beyond
> them a few steps out of the forest, one found a low hill, on which
> the reaped corn stood in stacks like the weapons of a vanished
> army, while across the sunken road, the abandoned fields,
> overgrown with broomsedge and life-everlasting, spread for several
> miles between worm fences which were half buried in brushwood.
> To the eyes of the stranger, fresh from the trim landscapes of
> England, there was an aspect of desolation in the neglected roads,
> in the deserted fields, and in the dim grey marshes beyond the low
> banks of the river. (5-6)

The failure of Jonathan, the antagonist of the plot (he competes with Abel for Molly's devotion), as lover and landowner is predicted here by his perception of the rural landscape as hostile; he does not belong in this environment where nature's force must be respected.

Another convention of plantation fiction that Glasgow alters is the love story. No longer concerned with a reconciliation theme, her early pastoral novels attempt to unite classes, not regions. Although Betty and Dan in *The Battle-Ground* both come from landowning families, Dan is the son of a renegade father. At the end of the novel the two lovers plan to farm together with the indication that they will use themselves, not slaves or tenants, for labor. Maria's and Christopher's union and Lila's marriage to a lower class farmer in *The Deliverance* also forecast a community of self-sufficient landowners. Molly's marriage to Abel in *The Miller of Old Church* celebrates the mixing of genteel stock (Molly's father was a Gay) with peasant blood.

By moving away from pastoralism toward agrarianism—from

plantation to yeoman farm—Glasgow is able to decentralize the romantic plot. Class structure becomes more important. She begins to focus more on the development of her heroines as part of the process of democratization, instead of as symbolic of the betrayed South, in the plantation romance genre. Although both Betty and Maria are "enablers" for the male heroes of *The Battle-Ground* and *The Deliverance*, at least their struggle for selfhood is described.

When Glasgow's female characters travel to the city, contrary to male characters, they return wiser and more appreciative of their country roots. Maria returns to the Blake plantation less refined and hardened by suffering but also more understanding of the value of the land. Molly's growth to self-knowledge is detailed in the plot. The reader follows her journey with the Gays while Abel's story is neglected. When the scene returns to Old Church it is more to reveal the tragedy of Judy Hatch, Abel's first wife, than to report his development. Abel remains essentially a static character.

In all three early pastorals the bad side of marriage offsets the final union of the protagonists. Early in *The Battle-Ground* the major unwittingly remarks: "When I hear a man talking about the abolition of slavery . . . I always expect him to want to do away with marriage next—" (63). Mrs. Blake makes a similarly ironic observation in *The Deliverance* when she tells Christopher, "I think marriage should be rightly regarded more as a duty than as a pleasure. I think it resembles more the selecting of a brand of flour" (201). Social obligation thus supersedes love. And, like the "mammy" figure in *Gone with the Wind* and *Sapphira and the Slave Girl*, the white southern lady is responsible for upholding patriarchal institutions.

Finally, in *The Miller of Old Church*, marriage is a trap Molly tries consciously to avoid until she acquiesces to Abel. He compares her evasion of him to a bird avoiding capture: "You've flown into my heart like a little bluebird in a cage, and there you'll beat and flutter, but you can't get out. Someday you'll rest there quiet, sweetheart" (207). Glasgow's imagery reveals more truth than her characters' conscious actions and words. We are not meant to view Abel as a potentially domineering or cruel husband, yet his "innocuous" comparison of Molly's state to a captured bird echoes the major's implicit comparison of marriage to slavery.

Molly's distrust of men is inherited from her mother, who was cruelly jilted by Jonathan's uncle when he refused to marry her and recognize her child as his. Aunt Kesiah tells the story: "When her trouble came she went quite out of her mind, perfectly harmless, I believe, and with lucid intervals in which she suffered from terrible melancholia" (84). Clearly, marriage is not presented as a positive state for women in these "romances." *The Miller of Old Church*, in fact, is Glasgow's last ostensible courtship plot before she centralizes the consequences of unhappy marriage in *Virginia* (1913) and *Life and Gabriella* (1916).

Glasgow reinforces her critique of the planter aristocracy by making her characters' response to the natural world an indication of their class bias. In general, the male characters, unless they are somehow "feminized" (like Christopher Blake or Abel Revercomb), read their own mental state into their surroundings. Mr. Ambler's view of his plantation is an example of this tendency. He sees a harmonious landscape when the world is ordered according to his wishes (the "outlying meadows seemed to reflect his gaze with a smile . . ."). After the war, he cannot see the desolation before him but instead, "his mind wandered again, and he talked in a low voice of the wheat fields at Uplands and of the cradles swinging all day in the sunshine" (415); this is an ironic vision for a man who claims he dislikes owning slaves. In *The Miller of Old Church* Jonathan Gay, especially, exhibits this tendency to associate landscape with his present mood. When he first encounters Blossom, the narrator reports:

> The melancholy of the landscape, reacting on the dangerous
> softness of his mood, bent his nature toward her like a flame
> driven by wind. Around them, in the red-topped orchard grass

faded to pale rose in the twilight, and beyond the crumbling rail
fence, miles of feathery broomsedge swept to the pines that stood
straight and black against the western horizon. Impressions of the
hour and scene, of colour and sound, were blended in the
allurement of the woman beside him. . . . (25)

How different is his reaction to nature here from what it is upon
his first sight of Old Church. Character replaces the narrator in
associating woman with the landscape.

Even Abel is sometimes guilty of misreading nature. When
Molly first accepts his offer of marriage, his eyes follow her as she
walks away:

. . . it seemed to him that the wan November day grew radiant with
colour, and that spring blossomed suddenly, out of season, over
the landscape. His hour was upon him when he turned and
retraced his steps over the silver brook and up the gradual slope,
where the sun shone on the bare soil and revealed each separate
clod of earth as if it were seen under a microscope. All nature was
at one with him. (179)

Of course this is a false view of nature, since winter is *not* a time of
renewal; consequently, Molly soon retracts her promise. Later when
Abel learns of Molly's inheritance from her father, again his emo-
tions cloud a genuine response to landscape: "His misery appeared
to him colossal, of a size that overshadowed, not only the spring
landscape, but life itself" (245).

The characters' false readings of nature are reinforced by the
portrayal of the cycle of seasons in each novel. Only in *The Battle-
Ground* do the lovers unite in spring, the season of renewal. The
two later novels end in autumn, and in this sense the natural
imagery becomes an ironic commentary on the reunion of the
couples.[4] In *The Deliverance* Maria comes to Christopher "across the
sunbeams" immediately after he looks out over the blazing landscape: "The air was strong with autumn scents, and as he drank it
in with deep drafts it seemed to him that he began to breathe
anew the spirit of life. . ." (543). Likewise, in *The Miller of Old Church*

Molly returns to Old Church in October and pledges her faithfulness to Abel later in the fall. In this closing scene, the narrator
emphasizes the "dead leaves" they walk over. As Molly waits for
Abel to appear, nature no longer gives her power and autonomy
but foreshadows the death of her freedom:

> A sudden blight had fallen over her, as if she had brought the
> presence of death with her out of that still chamber. Every sound
> was hushed into silence; every object appeared as unsubstantial as a
> shadow. Beyond the lawn, over the jewelled meadows, she could
> see the white spire of Old Church rising above the coloured foliage
> in the churchyard, and beyond it, lay the flat ashen turnpike,
> which had led hundreds of adventurous feet toward the great
> world they were seeking. She remembered that the sight of the
> turnpike had once made her restless; now it brought her only a
> promise of peace. (428–29)

In fact, for Glasgow's early female characters, nature always
eventually betrays and entraps them. Betty, Maria, and Molly learn
to "read" nature in order to accept the traditional roles it assigns
them. *The Battle-Ground* emphasizes nature's "restorative" properties; while in battle, Dan escapes his misery by imagining Betty
running over a field of flowers (324). Betty, too, can transcend her
daily hardship through a kind of "dual consciousness" that allows
her to be both with Dan and at the farm (328), yet instead of
seeing herself or her own experience in the landscape as the male
characters do, she empathizes with the natural world, pitying the
"naked elms" (99) or bringing corn for the starving crows (125).
Instead of projecting her identity on nature, she defines herself
through her interactions with it and thus ultimately can never
develop an independent self, only help Dan develop his.

Glasgow shifts this pattern somewhat in *The Deliverance*. She
makes Christopher, not Maria, the naturalized protagonist, and in
a sense, as Linda Wagner observes, he becomes the "heroine" of
the novel (30). Like Betty and Molly he is viewed as part of the

natural world or landscape; when Carraway arrives at Blake Hall he sees Christopher's figure in the fields at twilight:

> Farther away swept the freshly ploughed ground over which passed the moving figures of the labourers transplanting the young crop. Of them all, Carraway saw but a single worker . . . moulded physically perhaps in a finer shape than they, and limned in the lawyer's mental vision against a century of the brilliant if tragic history of his race. (12)

Subject to the "male gaze," Christopher must learn to obey its commands. This is why Maria becomes his "teacher" on how to become an *educated* yeoman farmer. By the end of the novel she has stamped him with a new identity, so that, far from despising his labor in the tobacco fields as he does in the opening pages, he needs to work out in the fresh air in order to restore his health.

But by "feminizing" Christopher, the author actually further marginalizes the female protagonist rather than liberating her from an entrapping bond with nature. Maria remains a disembodied heroine. She has no destiny to struggle against since the male hero has stolen her script. Her return to Blake Hall from the urban world serves one purpose in the plot—it enables the transfer of the plantation back to its "rightful" owners. As in the earlier pastoral, *The Battle-Ground*, marriage between the protagonists is assumed but never discussed in the novel.

After this experiment in switching gender roles, Glasgow returns to the naturalized heroine in her next pastoral, *The Miller of Old Church*. Like Betty, Molly identifies with animals and natural beauty, yet unlike her, she develops a stronger sense of self before succumbing to her female destiny as Abel's helpmate. Like Maria, Molly leaves the pastoral world in order to become "educated" in the city and returns to realize her "true love" for the novel's hero. However, Molly's acceptance of the simple rural world over Jonathan's city sophistication is both progressive and regressive; we at least witness her making a choice unlike Betty, who essentially has no choice. By choosing Abel, Molly loses the autonomy money would bring her. The urban world, however, still has restrictive codes for women as well. She submits to traditional subservience, yet perhaps this role will allow her some participation in the shaping of a new society, for as Abel's wife she will take part in the political process. Not for another fourteen years can Glasgow envision a woman character being an active part of the formation of the new yeoman class of farmers. With Dorinda in *Barren Ground*, the author not only abandons the marriage plot and focuses on female development but also allows her female protagonist an active voice in the community.

In these early pastorals, Glasgow demonstrates an interest in a new, more egalitarian society, yet just as her shift to independent women characters is incomplete, so is her critique of the old order. Aside from her obvious scorn of the slaveholding plantation masters, she never considers the continuation of black labor after the Civil War as problematic. The black characters in these novels remain rural spokespersons or comic figures. Likewise, although Pinetop, Dan's poor white battle companion, is granted a voice and sympathy in the plot of *The Battle-Ground*, he is never realized as an important character. The central figures of the plot are educated, if not also partly aristocratic (i.e., Dan, Maria, Molly). Nonetheless, the author's ironic treatment of the pastoral form and consequently of the feudal society it represents comes much earlier than many critics and readers assume.[5]

Glasgow's uneven development at this point in her career can be traced in a transitional character like Aunt Kesiah, who is both a victim of her role as a woman and of her class prejudice. A nascent "vein of iron" character, Kesiah had always wanted to be an artist and, according to her sister, the narcissistic Mrs. Gay, "it was out of the question that a Virginia lady should go off by herself and paint perfectly nude people in a foreign city" (75). The author's sympathy for her plight is clear:

> She remained what she had always been—a tragic perversion of
> nature which romance and realism conspired to ignore. Women in
> novels had revolted against life as passionately as she; but, one and
> all, they had revolted with graceful attitudes and with abundant
> braids or curls. (84)

Because she is ugly, Kesiah avoids the marriage trap, but there is
no alternative role for her to adopt, hence her bitterness toward
Molly who for awhile at least appears to have more freedom to act.
Kesiah's lack of understanding and sympathy for the lower classes
who essentially share her plight represents the crux of Glasgow's
critique. Unless the classes can comprehend each other's unique
problems, the society will not and cannot change. Until she spends
time with Molly, Kesiah expresses the typical view of the aristocracy
toward the poor whites. She remarks to Jonathan: "Before the war,
one scarcely ever heard of that class . . . it was so humble and
unpresuming; but in the last twenty-five or thirty years it has over-
run everything and most of the land about here has passed into its
possession" (84).

Unfortunately, although Kesiah may revise her opinion of Janet
Merryweather's daughter, she cannot rise above her own self-pity
to consider Molly's fate. As Jonathan approaches her to talk about
Molly's interest in Abel, Kesiah snips withered roses in the garden
(reminding the reader of her status as faded belle) and listens only
halfheartedly (374–75). Too much suffering has dulled her compassion, and a possible alliance with Molly remains unrealized.
Intergenerational and interclass female friendship is out of reach
for Glasgow at this stage in her artistic development, just as a fully
developed agrarian agenda remains outside the plot.

In *Barren Ground*, however, Glasgow successfully creates an alternative agrarian myth, launching a female pastoral tradition that
centers on woman as hero rather than as passive symbol of either
garden or earth.[6] To do this, the author must dismiss the significance of the old order. The opening pages of the novel detail the
difference between "good family," the effete aristocracy who still

insist upon "custom, history, tradition, romantic tradition fiction, and the Episcopal Church," and "good people," who "have their inconspicuous place in the social strata midway between the lower gentility and the upper class of 'poor white,' a position which encourages the useful rather than the ornamental public virtues" (5). In explaining the movement away from the country to the city by the sons of the good people, already the narrator suggests how the society might change. Only the old men and their daughters remain on the farm, and it is from the latter group that Glasgow constructs her plot. The author's intention, I believe, was to substitute a national myth, that of the yeoman farmer, for the localized oligarchic southern myth of her heritage.

Before establishing Dorinda as the novel's female hero, the author reviews her family history. The Abernethys, Dorinda's mother's family, were once plantation owners, the traditional subject of pastoral fiction, and the author invokes their past in order to reject it from her plot. The description of the plantation house occurs, as in Glasgow's earlier pastorals, as a means of criticizing the old order:

> In this long white house, encircled by the few cultivated fields in the midst of his still-virgin acres, John Calvin Abernethy lived with learning, prudence, and piety until he was not far from a hundred. He had but one son, for unlike the Scotch-Irish of the Valley, his race did not multiply. The son died in middle age, struck down by an oak he was felling, and his only child, a daughter [Dorinda's mother], was reared patiently but sternly by her grandfather. (8)

Significantly, the granddaughter marries Joshua Oakley, a poor white, and, like Molly Merryweather, enters a new social station. Unlike her predecessors Molly and Maria, however, Mrs. Oakley is not adept at farming and it takes another generation before her daughter Dorinda can begin to embody the yeoman farmer ideal Glasgow advocates. By examining Dorinda's management of her farm and her mastery of the broomsedge, one can see how she transforms the pastoral myth from a male- to a female-centered quest for heroism. To accomplish this, she changes the characters' relationship to the land and the representation of the land as female.

Dorinda's heroic quest to save her family's farm after her father's death is in fact a radical plot for southern women authors of this era. For the most part they focus on the woman protagonist (if indeed there is one) as either too entrapped by her role as belle or too poor to realize how to overcome the drudgery of tenant farming. Francis Newman's *The Hard-Boiled Virgin* (1926), for instance, depicts a woman who refuses the role of marriage—the prescribed goal of the "belle"— but only through denying her sexuality altogether. Elizabeth Madox Roberts's Ellen Chesser in *The Time of Man*, published the same year, is more aware and accepting of her sexuality as she grows up in harmony with the natural world; however, she is thwarted from developing autonomy by the harsh existence of subsistence farming. Even Edna Ferber's contemporary *So Big*, winner of the 1925 Pulitzer Prize in fiction, depicts its heroine, Selina DeJong, not so much as successful farmer as devoted and self-sacrificing mother. Selina, in some senses Dorinda's midwestern counterpart, does not have to struggle against the strictures of southern society. She has only to translate the agrarian ideal from a male to a female model.

Still, Glasgow's and Ferber's women protagonists share some characteristics that are important to note in novels of this time period. Both value and are fulfilled through work instead of marriage. Conveniently, Selina's husband dies early so that she can experiment with new farming methods and improve her land's yield without having to confront his authority. Dorinda, likewise, is head of the household and directs Nathan almost as if he were a hired hand on her land. Fortunately, he agrees with her about new farming techniques, but her land ownership also gives her the prerogative to decide how the land will be cultivated.

Glasgow's novel goes further than Ferber's, however, in rejecting the romantic plot so central to pastoral fiction. Rather than absenting the male figure entirely to allow the female protagonist autonomous development (as with Betty in *The Battle-Ground*), she transforms the marriage relationship. First, just as the plantation house and family must be invoked before dismissing them, the romantic plot must also be rejected. The author's previous novel, *Life and Gabriella*, ends with the heroine accepting a new suitor even after she has successfully supported her son through her work as a millner. As Rachel Blau Du Plessis points out, until after World War I most women novelists conformed to this prescribed ending of marriage or death (1–19). Glasgow's rejection of this script, therefore, represents a radical departure from the contemporary female plot. *Barren Ground*'s love story ends a third of the way through the novel after Jason seduces and jilts Dorinda. Although through much of the rest of the novel Dorinda seems bent on revenge, at least she is able to overcome male betrayal and establish a new life. She is not ostracized by the community but earns respect for herself through her successful farming.

Second, by marrying Nathan, Dorinda secures social respectability and avoids conjugal responsibility. As step-mother Dorinda can have the satisfaction of guiding John Abner and enjoying his companionship without succumbing to the dangerous, irrational "mother love" her mother felt for Rufus.

Furthermore, like Alexandra's relationship with Carl in Willa Cather's *O Pioneers!* (1913), Dorinda's and Nathan's bond is one of friendship instead of passion and thus far more sustaining. The two share a love for the land and fulfillment through labor on it. As passionate as her desire for Jason had been, Dorinda realizes that Nathan is the better man. After buying the Greylock land, the two sit on the porch together watching the shooting stars, and Dorinda thinks to herself, "He is worth twenty of Jason," but she cannot say the words aloud and fails in her effort "to say something affectionate" (404–5).

The language of friendship has not yet developed between

male and female protagonists. Glasgow has no model to follow in depicting this scene. This one intimate moment is an important understatement in the plot, however, for it indicates a new direction for the pastoral genre. No longer a sexual battle for possession, land and its cultivation become the mutual interest. The imagery in this scene confirms the significance of a new kind of relationship: "Whenever she looked back on it afterwards, it seemed to lie there like a fertile valley in the arid monotony of her life" (405).

Dorinda does pay a large price for her freedom and for this friendship—the loss of a sexually intimate marriage—yet as the imagery of *Barren Ground* reveals, she finds compensation for this lost sexuality. By making Dorinda respond to and overcome the broomsedge, Glasgow can represent the sexual battle between men and women without submitting her protagonist to the female destiny. A direct portrayal of passion would be too dangerous for the female heroic plot. A complete denial of it, however, would sacrifice verisimilitude and make Dorinda more like Alexandra, an almost mythic character. Cather's protagonist's relationship to the land is subtly different from her successor's. Alexandra is strengthened by a mystical union with the earth, but it is not a sexual relationship as this encounter of Dorinda's clearly is meant to be:

> The storm and the hag-ridden dreams of the night were over, and the land which she had forgotten was waiting to take her back to its heart. Endurance. Fortitude. The spirit of the land was flowing into her, and her own spirit, strengthened and refreshed, was flowing out again toward life. . . . Again she felt the quickening of that sympathy which was deeper than all other emotions of her heart, which love had overcome only for an hour and life had been powerless to conquer in the end,—the living communion with the earth under her feet. . . . (524)

Nevertheless, the land here clearly does *not* substitute for or become a male presence; it is *not* gendered. Dorinda's fulfillment comes from work, and her erotic relationship with the land suggests another possibility for the female protagonist—as for the male hero, romance becomes secondary to the heroic quest.

But by keeping Dorinda susceptible to passion whether it is deflected to her desire to possess land or not, Glasgow cannot completely erase all vestiges of the romantic pastoral plot. Like her successor Scarlett O'Hara in *Gone with the Wind*, Dorinda steals the role of hero from the male characters and she must "atone" for this sin. First, no one recognizes her heroic acts. While she is credited for being a successful farmer by the community, as soon as a more conventional "heroic" event occurs, Dorinda loses the spotlight. Nathan's death provides Pedlar's Mill the opportunity to give the traditional accolades to a "proper" hero. At his funeral and afterwards, he is saluted for his daring rescue of suffering women from the train wreck, no matter that his act was foolish. Chivalry fits the society's code better than the courage of defying customs. Dorinda resents the cheap sentiment that the community, which had never respected Nathan while he was alive, expends over his death. But her scorn of this "legendizing" hides her own jealousy of his recognition: "She felt ashamed of herself. Had she failed Nathan in his death because she could not recognize him in what she thought of vaguely as his heroic part?" (453). And as the adulation for Nathan continues, she thinks secretly, "Yes, it was something, Dorinda assured her rebellious heart, to have been married to a hero" (471). For this reason, as much as her growing sense of autonomy, Dorinda determines not to marry again. She is tired of men receiving all the glory.

Another vestige of the pastoral plot is the female as enabler, exemplified by Betty in *The Battle-Ground*. Although Dorinda is not Nathan's or Jason's enabler, she does take care of her former lover while he is on his deathbed as a kind of "atonement" for her "sin" of rebelling from the role of the ruined heroine. Like Jezebel in the 1938 film of the same name, she must pay homage to the "hero" by sharing his suffering.

Dorinda's inability to form alliances/friendships with other women is, in fact, a setback for Glasgow in reshaping the pastoral plot. In *The Miller of Old Church*, Molly reaches out to Blossom in her pain of Jonathan's neglect, and the narrator comments:

> The relation of woman to man was dwarfed suddenly by an understanding of the relationship of woman to woman. Deeper than the dependence of sex, simpler, more natural, closer to the earth, as if it still drew its strength from the soil . . . the need of woman for woman was not written in the songs and the histories of men, but in the neglected and frustrated lives which the songs and the histories of men had ignored. (410)

Conversely, although unlike Molly, Dorinda is able to develop autonomy and free herself from the female destiny, she is not able to identify with others in the society who face the same oppression.

The only relationship she has that approaches female friendship is with her maid, Fluvanna. Midway through the novel the narrator reports:

> The affection between the two women had outgrown the slender tie of mistress and maid, and had become as strong and elastic as the bond that holds relatives together. They knew each other's daily lives; they shared the one absorbing interest in the farm. . . . (349)

Dorinda's attitude toward Fluvanna suffers from "an inherited feeling of condescension," as Elizabeth Schultz notes (70–71), yet this relationship, though never enacted through dialogue, becomes an important sustenance for the protagonist after Nathan's death. Again, as for heterosexual friendship, the author has not developed a language for the two women to use; neither racial nor sexual barriers to friendship have been crossed.

Consequently, Glasgow's pastoral world in *Barren Ground* allows individual triumph. Dorinda successfully embodies the author's yeoman farmer ideal, yet it is not clear how others are to follow her example—whether women or men, black or white. Abandoning her goal of agrarian reform, the author creates a female hero

who defies literary convention by becoming her own rescuer. She
also begins to imagine ways in which the society as a whole can
redesign itself to eliminate hierarchies of class and race. The nascent friendships between Dorinda and Nathan and Dorinda and
Fluvanna represent her attempt to shift the plot even further from
the traditional pastoral. In 1925, however, especially in the South,
it is still too difficult to visualize these relationships as completely
equal.

Ten years later, Glasgow published her final pastoral novel,
Vein of Iron, which in some ways retreats from this new pastoral
vision of female autonomy. Ada Fincastle is neither as self-assured
nor ambitious as Dorinda. The novel, however, is problematic
rather than regressive. Glasgow is in some ways more ambitious in
redefining the genre, but the risks she takes are not fully realized
in the plot. Although the Fincastles return to Ironside at the end
in order to recapture the old life they had led, they do so to regain
autonomy and to farm side by side instead of maintaining the
gender specialized roles required by the industrialized society.

In this final rural novel, the contrast between city and country
is sharpest. The manse and the small village of Ironside ultimately
represent all that is good in civilization, even though earlier Ada,
the protagonist, must escape the rural community and the oppro-
brium of unmarried motherhood. As Judy Smith Murr points out,
the city of Queenborough serves the same purpose in this novel as
the broomsedge in *Barren Ground*: it represents sterility and paraly-
sis (52). The "pastoral," in the conventional sense of nostalgic,
idealized vision, is certainly strongest in this late novel, written
when Glasgow was in her sixties. But to overlook the *way* in which
the rural world is idealized is to miss the overall implications of the
novel as a revision of the genre.

Envisioning an Appalachian community that had never depended on slave labor, the author can reshape gender portrayals
less problematically.[7] Glasgow pictures a past community that is
matriarchal and self-sufficient rather than hierarchical and patriar-

chal as the plantation society had been represented in literature. Ada's family, the Fincastles, claims not an aristocratic heritage, like Dorinda's, but a pioneer one.

And the most notable ancestors, as Ada's grandmother relates, are women. In the collective family memory, stories of brave women battling the "savages" are more common than tales of male heroism. Ada's grandmother tells about "Mrs. Ettrick, a woman of great strength . . . surprised by a redskin. . . . [S]he felled him with the single blow of a hatchet and galloped back to warn the men . . ." (21). Later in the novel, Ada, outcast and pregnant with Ralph's child, recalls these stories about her heroic female foremothers:

> Mrs. Morecock had seen the brains of her baby spatter her skirts; she had been famished for food as a captive; she had eaten roots; when she reached water, she had knelt down and lapped it up like an animal. In the end she had had the courage to escape, she had crossed trackless mountains on her way home to Ironside. . . . Though she was a walking skeleton when she reached Ironside, she had the spirit, or the folly, to begin life again. . . . How could they drop the past so easily, those pioneers, and plunge into the moment before them? They were hard, it was true, but it was the hardness of character. Unlovable they were, but heroic. . . . (248)

Ada's discomfort with a female heroic role is evident here; the story suggests that autonomous action and love are incompatible. Nonetheless, unlike Dorinda, whose only legend of heroism is Nathan's, this later Glasgow protagonist has women models. Richard Slotkin and Leslie Fiedler have identified the importance of Indian war and captivity narratives in the development of western frontier mythology. Indian captivity runs through the southern pastoral tradition as an important subplot underlining female helplessness.[8] Perhaps Glasgow is defining here a female western hero much as her contemporary Elizabeth Madox Roberts does in her historical romance *The Great Meadow* (1930).[9]

More likely, however, as Annette Kolodny points out, since women's frontier fantasies were different from their conquering

male counterparts' (*The Land Before Her* 161), the author is recall-
ing a different model. Captivity narratives by women served other
purposes, as Chris Castiglia explains:

> The continued fascination of the captivity narrative for female
> authors . . . indicates a common female experience beyond literal
> abduction by Indians. . . . [T]he captivity narrative has offered
> women a site for struggling with the complex issues of inscribing
> a female subject . . . a symbolic economy for expressing their
> dissatisfaction with the roles and scripts offered by the patriarchy.

Glasgow uses the Indian captivity narrative to emphasize the
denial of women's sexuality or "wildness." Ada's great-great-grandmother, Martha Tod, had lived with the Shawnees for seven years
and had been married to a young chief (17). Returning to white
society, Martha Tod never completely readapts to its mores even
after her marriage to one of the church elders but suffers "from
spells of listening, a sort of wildness, which would steal upon her in
the fall of the year, especially in the blue haze of weather they
called Indian summer. Then she would leap up at the hoot of an
owl or the bark of a fox and disappear into the forest . . ." (41–42).
It is even rumored that on her deathbed, "her youth, with the old
listening look had flashed back into her face, and she had tried to
turn toward the forest" (42).

Like her great-great-grandmother, Ada has a streak of "wildness" which causes her to identify with the Indians. She dreams
often of escaping to the Indian trail to be with Ralph, and when he
returns on leave this is indeed where they go for their secret tryst.
Instead of drawing power—and sexual fulfillment—from the earth,
as Dorinda does, Ada looks to the mountains. Jan Zlotnik Schmidt
suggests that the two mountains that overshadow Ironside represent two sides of Ada's temperament: God's Mountain is her romantic idealization of love, and Thunder Mountain, where Martha
Tod was taken captive, and where Ada and Ralph go to find the
Indian Trail, is the dark side of love (132–33). On Thunder Mountain, like Charity Royall of Edith Wharton's *Summer* (1917) who

escapes to the mountains with her lover, Ada discovers both her heritage and her repressed sexuality.

In Ironside, and even more so in Queenborough, neither can be expressed. While Glasgow does not deny Ada's sexuality, according to Julius Raper it must exist outside of time and space, and Ada is made to pay for its consequences with a bastard child (*From the Sunken Garden* 167). What is important to emphasize here is that Ada's "affair" with Ralph is her choice. She is neither seduced like earlier Glasgow heroines nor too young to understand the transitory nature of passion as Dorinda is. The author allows her *adult* passion undisguised by land imagery (as in *Barren Ground*). Yet despite Ada's conscious decision to break the moral code of her Calvinistic society, her sense of guilt underlies all of Part III (appropriately titled "Life's Interlude") as Ralph continually urges her "not to think" about the punishment she may have to pay.[10] According to Kathryn Lee Seidel, this sexual guilt indicates a major theme of Glasgow's later fiction: acknowledging sexuality becomes a greater stumbling block for her women protagonists than the restricting traditions of southern society themselves. (82).

Again, the author expresses this ambivalence through imagery borrowed from the captivity narrative. After Ralph's accident and while he is still in the hospital, Ada has a nightmare in which she dreams:

> She was running from Indians up the stony hillside at the back of the manse. As a Shawnee in war paint pursued her, she dodged behind big gray rocks, up, up, up, always with her heart in her throat and her breath whistling from terror, springing, stooping, bending, crawling, fleeing, until at last a tomahawk whirled down at her from the other side of a stone, and while she waited for the crash into her skull, the painted face of the Indian turned into a sheep—into the benign feature of the old ewe that had gazed at her over the stalk of mullein. (332–33)

The images of the dream conflate many anxieties. While the threat the Indian represents is unclear, Ada's terror of him indicates her

fear of entrapment; her active fleeing reverses her conscious feelings of helplessness and passivity as a result of Ralph's accident.
Significantly, the tomahawk is hurled almost as if from an unknown source. Again, as for her ancestor Martha Tod, Indians are
not just evil captors—they become here "a benign feature," a means
of returning to the rural manse imaginatively if not literally. More
important, running from the Indians, Ada is running from sexual
pursuit. Had she not gone with Ralph up the mountain to the
Indian trail years earlier, she would not have to face his sexual
betrayal later. Sexual liberation for women clearly does not free
them from the double standard that men still practice.

The consequences and dangers of either expressing or re-
pressing one's sexuality are also intimated elsewhere in the plot.
From the opening scene when Ada feels empathy for the idiot
child Toby Waters, the reader is exposed to the ugly effects of
incest. Although Ladell Payne notes the "cosmic symbolism" of
this imagery (64), Glasgow means to convey more than an existen-
tial message here. For society, and for women especially, the consequences of sexuality—disguised as "romance" in the typical plot
complication of the pastoral—can be devastating.

Written in the turbulent thirties, this novel reflects the tensions women felt as a result of breaking free from prescribed roles
a decade earlier. Ada can recognize and act on her sexual desires,
but she is still ashamed of them. And the author's portrayal of
other women characters in the novel shows ambivalence toward
this "sexual liberation": both Janet and Minna abuse sex. Janet
uses it as a tool for power (forcing a shotgun marriage with Ralph),
and Minna embodies the Southern belle-bitch dichotomy with her
malicious flirting. Glasgow's portrayal of these characters suggests
the contradictory view women were subject to during the depres-
sion; one year later (1936), Scarlett O'Hara appears on the literary
scene to epitomize the stereotype of the corrupted southern belle.

Imagistically, Ada's failure to overcome her dependence on
emotion and her punishment for her sexuality result from her

separation from the elemental forces of nature (as in her nightmare of the pursuing Indians). Never directly identifying with the
earth, Ada remains trapped by the romantic plot and seeks Ralph's
approval, unlike Dorinda who transcends her dependence on men
through work on her farm. In *Vein of Iron* it is John Fincastle, Ada's
father, who works with his hoe in order to console himself and
gain perspective on his life. According to Linda Wagner, Glasgow
identifies as much with Ada's father as she does with her female
protagonist (97).

Still, in creating a stable rural community which depends on
extended matriarchal families, Glasgow continues her program of
revising southern society. As sentimental and conventional as Ada's
and Ralph's reconciliation is at the end of the novel, it represents
a step forward in resolving the sexual battle of the pastoral world.
In a sense, as Schmidt observes, Ada and Ralph become a new
Adam and Eve "to emerge from the ashes of modern civilization,
vivify a survival ethic, and construct a new pastoral world and a
redemptive legend . . ." (131). Dorinda must treat her husband
Nathan and all men who interact with her essentially as hired
hands; an emotional/physical relationship would threaten her autonomy. Ada, conversely, accepts motherhood and subservience to
her husband but still remains faithful to her maternal heritage of
pioneer strength. Motherhood also enables her to produce a new
generation of rural survivors, unlike Dorinda whose triumph is
essentially individual.

Toward the end of her career, Glasgow sees the return to rural
values as the only way society can help solve the growing problem
of urban displacement and poverty. She focuses here on the poor
whites and only briefly considers the plight of the rest of society.
Aunt Abigail, the Fincastles' black servant, shares work and old
age with Ada's grandmother. Yet, like Fluvanna in *Barren Ground*,
she is more an enabler for the family rather than a recognizable
character. Again, as in the earlier novel, some members of society
succeed at the cost of others. Julius Raper observes that in *Vein*, as in

many of Glasgow's novels, "panoramas of periods" and dissections
of society are secondary to "novels of character" (*From the Sunken
Garden* 161). The development of other characters is ignored for
the sake of Ada's self-realization.

Glasgow, nevertheless, clearly wants Ada and Ralph to overcome their differences and to lead a productive, *shared* life in
Ironside, though she cannot quite visualize it in the plot. Linda
Wagner suggests that, unlike her earlier novels which conclude
optimistically and indicate new directions for society, "*Vein of Iron* is
truly a novel about the way all human beings must live" (108).
There can be no individual triumph for her female protagonist;
community replaces individualism in this novel. The author states
in its preface: "I was trying to isolate, not a single character or
group of characters alone, but the vital principle of survival" (qtd.
in Wagner 102–3). In Queenborough, Ada and Aunt Meggie are as
concerned for their neighbors' welfare as for their own family's. In
the urban world, as we will see with Harriette Arnow's Gertie
Nevels, they learn the cooperative structures that they will transfer
to their rural homeland. In this sense, Glasgow's late return to the
pastoral form represents both a more realistic assessment of male-
female relationships and a recognition of the importance of communal values.[11]

This pastoral vision is paradoxically both a drastic departure
from and a reaffirmation of tensions in the author's early work.
Glasgow's first published fiction, "A Woman of Tomorrow," a story
that appeared in *Short Stories* in 1895, presents the protagonist's dilemma between "love and ambition"—romantic plot versus bil-
dungsroman—that essentially informs all her work. In an early
scene before the young hero leaves her rural Virginia to become a
lawyer in the city, the narrator depicts a typical pastoral scene
followed by the hero's rejection of it:

> Upon an adjacent hill a group of hayricks stood out forlornly in
> the landscape. A pale ray of sunshine shifted uneasily over them,
> casting violet-toned shadows at their feet and touching their yellow

crests with the promise of a benediction that could never be
fulfilled. . . . It seemed to Patricia, standing there, that she herself,
with her young strength and troubled eyes, belonged to another
scene, another age. Upon the fence beside her a whippoorwill
alighted, watching her with shrewd, suspicious eyes. Yes, she
belonged elsewhere—she, a woman of the twentieth century. Even
nature seemed distrustful of her here—where she was encircled by
phantoms of the past. . . .
(2–3)[12]

Until *Barren Ground*, nature and female character are at odds in
Glasgow; "the promise of a benediction that could never be fulfilled" warns the reader that Patricia cannot find happiness in this
rural landscape, and indeed, the description of her that follows
foreshadows her departure from it. At the end of the story, however, the female hero cannot so easily "tread ruthlessly upon
lovevine and clover" (7) without finally facing the loneliness her
career costs her.

Returning ten years later to visit the man she might have
married, Patricia finds that he has a wife, "a small, tired woman in
a soiled gown, with a child upon her shrunken breast" (13). Although she "walk[ed] rapidly away" to watch the sunset and
"stretched out her arms with a gesture of thankfulness," she then
"burst into tears,"—an action that Julius Raper interprets as "the
disenchantment of reality" (14). Her tears, I believe, are not so
much disappointment as relief and indicate here how the Glasgow
female hero escapes the prescribed plot through rejecting her
rural heritage. *Vein of Iron*, of course, represents the opposite move–
ment. Ada returns to rural Ironside, yet it is to affirm new possibility. As in *Barren Ground*, romance is superseded by friendship. Ralph
and Ada are no longer lovers. But because they will now work on
the land together, they can be partners instead of becoming estranged.

Glasgow's pastoral vision has evolved from woman as enabler
to woman as enabled through her relationship to the land. Simi-

larly, the next pastoral to be considered, Margaret Mitchell's *Gone with the Wind*, also changes the dichotomy between love and self-realization. Scarlett O'Hara's return to Tara at the end of the novel represents not defeat or retreat from society but rather an affirmation of the female pastoral plot—a regenerative bonding with the land.

2. Margaret Mitchell's Feminist Farm Fantasy: *Gone with the Wind*

Only her feeling for Tara had not changed. . . . Her love
for . . . this beautiful red earth that was blood colored, garnet,
brick starred with white puffs, was one part of Scarlett which
did not change when all else was changing. . . . When she
looked at Tara she could understand, in part, why wars were
fought. Rhett was wrong when he said men fought wars for
money. No, they fought for . . . the red earth which was theirs
and would be their sons', the red earth which would bear
cotton for their sons and their sons' sons. . . . Yes, Tara was
worth fighting for, and she accepted simply and without
question the fight. No one was going to get Tara away from
her. No one was going to set her and her people adrift on the
charity of relatives. She would hold Tara, if she had to break
the back of every person on it.

—*Gone with the Wind*

Like Ellen Glasgow's Dorinda Oakley and Ada Fincastle, Scarlett
O'Hara returns to the land in *Gone with the Wind* (*GWTW*) in order
to recover her strength and identity. Margaret Mitchell's protagonist, however, is not often noted for her farming abilities.[1] Critics
stress her headstrong determination and female heroism without
closely examining their source, for Scarlett does more than "steal
the script" from the typical white southern male hero of the plantation legend tradition.[2] Her female quest for power differs from
the male version since she has no "legitimate" means to pursue or
inherit it.

I argue, however, that despite Scarlett's heroic qualities—notable in a woman brought up under the system of southern chiv-

alry—she resembles more William Faulkner's earth mother figures
like Lena Grove and Eula Varner than Willa Cather's or Ellen
Glasgow's female heroes. For all her willfulness, Scarlett remains
essentially a static character, her drive for power less a conscious
desire to assume a new role in society than an attempt to recreate
the old order she unconsciously rebels from.

Furthermore, Scarlett's success is based upon a callous disregard for the lives of others around her— including her sisters, her
children, and most glaringly, her black slaves. Mitchell's use of a
historical setting does *not* make such a critique of the novel's racism anachronistic. As Helen Taylor has argued, *GWTW* presents the
1930s' neo-Confederate cause. Taylor explains how "Mitchell uses
Reconstruction as the great unifying and consolidating historical
crisis for southern whites. While the war divides and destroys families, breaking down traditional class, gender and race relations,
Reconstruction restores white southern confidence . . ." (125).
The novel, in other words, becomes propaganda for the Jim Crow
society of a pre–civil rights South.

Nevertheless, once these problematic aspects of the novel are
acknowledged, it can be included in a study of the female pastoral
because, despite her lack of consciousness and communality, Scarlett exemplifies a woman protagonist whose identity is shaped by
her relationship to the land and who learns to empower herself
through this bond. Aside from its neo-Confederate purpose,
GWTW explores new gender roles for Mitchell's contemporaries.
Anne Goodwyn Jones notes that popular women authors of the
1930s use history as a function of gender, unlike male authors who
imagine gender roles within their historical contexts (*"Gone with the
Wind* and Others" 364). By doing so, these women authors do not
rewrite the plantation legend they inherit. Rather, they change its
substructure from a defense of an oligarchic order to a study of
the characters, particularly the white women, within that order.

The antebellum women in *GWTW* are, as Elizabeth Fox-
Genovese explains, actually disguises for the "flappers" and "new

women" of Mitchell's own generation. Stereotypical southern belles are devalued in favor of *active* women who represent the values of a postwar society ("Scarlett O'Hara: The Southern Lady as New Woman," 399–401). Scarlett and her sisters, like Glasgow's white southern women in *The Deliverance*, represent a split in the character traits associated with the white southern lady. Scarlett embodies her mother's managing capabilities and authoritative presence while her younger sisters, particularly young Carreen, are docile and demure. After the war, Carreen's weak constitution renders her more and more ethereal, hardly a character at all. Suellen's protests against her older sister's inflexible rule make Scarlett appear narrow-minded and selfish, the typical narcissist of twentieth-century plantation fiction.[3]

Ellen O'Hara represents the old ideal of white southern womanhood in the novel. Hers is the claim for family pedigree: her parents were French aristocrats escaping from Haiti. Yet significantly, when the narrator introduces her in the novel, she already seems outdated and ghostlike. At thirty-two "according to the standards of her day, she was a middle-aged woman," and "(s)he would have been a strikingly beautiful woman had there been any glow in her eyes, any responsive warmth in her smile. . ." (42). Yet she is established from the moment she appears in Tara's entryway as the head of the household.

Although Scarlett is forever attempting to live up to her mother's example and thinks of her as she does the Virgin Mary, she herself, as Rhett often reminds her, is no "lady." Mitchell reveals in her voluminous correspondence after the novel's publication that her purpose was not to memorialize the antebellum South: "I don't mean that I wrote a sweet, sentimental novel of the Thomas Nelson Page type. My central woman character does practically everything that a lady of the old school should not do. . . ." (5). Thus, *GWTW* is *not* simply a twentieth-century version of the plantation romance. By rejecting the central mythic structure of the virtuous white southern lady, the flower of the aristocratic

garden, the novel begins to dismantle the southern pastoral world.
The novel is not as ambivalent about the past as many critics claim.
Instead, as we will see, by revising and reversing gender roles and
positing a female over a male hero, it rejects the code of chivalry
central to southern society.

Not only does Scarlett occupy the place of the male hero in
the plot, the novel itself centers on her consciousness, however
unselfconscious and self-deceptive.[4] The omniscient narrator
privileges Scarlett's viewpoint. She and not Rhett—who after all
abandons her on the journey to Tara—portrays the characteristics
of the typical questing male hero. First, she is treated by her father
as the eldest "son." He imbues in her respect for the land and
desire for property acquisition. He scolds her in the very first
scene with an admonition that she remembers long afterwards:
"Land is the only thing in the world that amounts to anything . . .
for 'tis the only thing in the world that lasts, and don't you be
forgetting it! . . ." (38–39). Second, aside from Rhett, Scarlett is the
most active and successful character in the novel. She saves Tara
from being sold, supports her own and Ashley's family, and builds
a booming sawmill enterprise from Frank's modest business.

This activism, in fact, separates her from both male and female roles in the southern pastoral. Not a passive southern lady,
neither is she a genteel aristocrat. From her father, a self-made
immigrant from Ireland, she inherits a fiery temper and a lack of
qualms about business associates. She will deal with anyone who
strikes a good bargain, whether Yankee or cracker, thereby violating the southern chivalric code and threatening class hierarchy.[5]

Part of *GWTW*'s immense appeal may be its inscription of the
national myth of rags-to-riches using a southern setting. Readers
are given a paradoxical combination of southern pride and national patriotism in the O'Hara family history. Gerald arrives on
American soil with only "the clothes he had on his back, two
shillings above his passage money and a price on his head that he
felt was larger than his misdeed warranted" (44). Not exactly a
Horatio Alger figure, he wins Tara in a poker game instead of

through virtuous hard work. Nonetheless, Gerald achieves the American dream of wealth with luck and resourcefulness, again a pattern Scarlett imitates after the war. Father and daughter are still not guaranteed a place in southern society as a result of their economic triumph. Both aspire to the southern dream of aristocracy without realizing that one cannot "buy" class position.[6]

Scarlett's heroic traits of energy, determination, and action are not, however, acquired solely from her father. Heroism is not, as in the traditional southern pastoral, equated with masculinity. Appropriately, in a novel that replaces a male with a female hero, the protagonist's role models are women. It is Scarlett's mother, not her father, who is really in charge of Tara, and it is she who exhibits courage by defying her family's wishes to risk marriage to an unknown man from "uncivilized" north Georgia. She sets out on a completely unknown journey to a new world. This streak of daring can in fact be traced back to Scarlett's Grandma Robillard, whom Scarlett describes to Rhett as: "cold as an icicle and strict about her manners and everybody's else's manners, but she married three times and had any number of duels fought over her and she wore rouge and the most shockingly low-cut dresses . . ." (672). Biographer Anne Edwards reports that, in fact, Mitchell's protagonist was modeled not only on the author's own characteristic headstrong nature, but also on that of her grandmother. The matrilineal heritage of the novel repeats an actual inheritance.[7]

Two other women characters serve as role models for Scarlett: Beatrice Tarleton and Grandma Fontaine. The former is "[f]rail, fine-boned, [and] so white of skin that her flaming hair seemed to have drawn all the color from her face," but also "possessed of exuberant health and untiring energy" (87). She raises eight children, manages a plantation, and breeds fine horses—all without mention of a husband. Arriving at the Wilkes's barbecue in the opening scene, she holds the reins on the family's carriage. She is literally a "matriarch," although she remains an aberration in a patriarchal society.

Grandma Fontaine is a more problematic mentor. She coun-

sels Scarlett on two important occasions, the first soon after Scarlett
returns to Tara to find it ravaged by northern soldiers. After discussing the plight of various neighbors and lending Scarlett food,
she tells the younger woman how she once survived an Indian
attack as an illustration both of courage and submission:

> . . . I lay there and saw our house burn and I saw the Indians scalp
> my brothers and sisters. . . . And they dragged Mother out and
> killed her about twenty feet from where I was lying. . . . And in the
> morning I set out for the nearest settlement and it was thirty miles
> away. It took me three days to get there through the swamps and
> the Indians, and afterward they thought I'd lose my mind. . . .
> That's where I met Dr. Fontaine. He looked after me. . . [S]ince
> that time I've never been afraid of anything or anybody because I'd
> known the worst that could happen to me. And that lack of fear
> has gotten me into a lot of trouble and cost me a lot of happiness.
> God intended women to be timid frightened creatures and there's
> something unnatural about a woman who isn't afraid. . . . Scarlett,
> always save something to fear—even as you save something to
> love. . . . (446)

As in Ellen Glasgow's *Vein of Iron* (1935), this frontier narrative encodes the bravery of women while it simultaneously juxtaposes
American pioneer myth with southern legend. Grandma Fontaine's courage is offset by her dependence on male rescue just as
Scarlett's later economic independence is compromised by emotional dependence and exploitation of a system that, like the white
takeover of Indian territory, disregards the rights of others.

Scarlett's second encounter with Grandma Fontaine reveals
even more clearly the danger of substituting female for male
"heroism." The placement of this scene in the novel is important
for it occurs *before* Scarlett's marriage to Rhett, that is, before she is
tutored by him in the ways of climbing to power. After Gerald
O'Hara's funeral, Mrs. Fontaine shares her philosophy of survival
with Scarlett:

We bow to the inevitable. We're not wheat, we're buckwheat!
When a storm comes along it flattens ripe wheat because it's dry
and can't bend with the wind. But ripe buckwheat's got sap in it
and it bends. And when the wind has passed, it springs up almost
as straight and strong as before. We aren't a stiff-necked tribe. . . .
When trouble comes we bow to the inevitable without any
mouthing, and we work and we smile and we bide our time. And
we play along with lesser folks and we take what we can get from
them. And when we're strong enough, we kick the folks whose
necks we've climbed over. That, my child, is the secret of the
survival. (709–10)

Here Scarlett is first given "permission" to use others in her climb
to power. The novel never calls into question this kind of destructive heroism or offers another kind. By transferring rather than
transforming character traits, Mitchell continues to defend rather
than criticize a system that favors individual competition over community. Grandma Fontaine's rugged individualism is the same as
Gerald's. Neither models the kind of interdependent rural society
Glasgow envisions in *Vein of Iron.*[8]

Thus, unlike her contemporary southern women authors,
Mitchell never completely re-visions the male pastoral to create a
female-centered form. Because the central motif of the southern
pastoral is virgin land, the only way to become a hero in this genre
is to *be* male. As much as Mitchell challenges assigned gender roles
through Scarlett's quest for power and survival, she also continues
the traditional representation of the land as female, and consequently her protagonist cannot transform the male heroic quest
into a female one.

The imagery of the land and the characters' relationship to it
make clear Scarlett's underlying ambivalence toward her own autonomy and underline her inability to assume completely the role
of the male hero. In *GWTW,* as in the traditional southern pastoral, land represents both the white southern lady and the South
itself. The southern male has proprietary rights over both. Only he

is allowed to decide whether to protect and preserve the earth's "virginity" or to "possess" it through cultivation.

In the opening scene of the novel, Mitchell describes north Georgia as a land of contrasts, newly settled, where "the virgin forests . . . mysterious, a little sinister . . . seemed to wait with an age-old patience, to threaten with soft sighs: 'Be careful! Be careful! We had you once. We can take you back again'" (10). Land, like woman, is inherently untamed, arcane; it must be cultivated carefully with an ever-watchful eye. Even more telling is Mitchell's description of the freshly plowed fields:

> . . . the bloody glory of the sunset colored the fresh cut furrows of the red Georgia clay to even redder hues. The moist hungry earth, waiting upturned for the cotton seeds, showed pinkish on the sandy tops of furrows, vermilion and scarlet and maroon where shadows lay along the sides of the trenches. . . . (10)

Here, as in all pastorals, the representation of the land is crucial because it determines the nature of the conflict. As long as the landscape is imagined as gendered—it is clearly female in *GWTW*—the plot becomes a battle for dominance rather than a struggle for self-empowerment. The female landscape in southern pastoral is different from the kind Ellen Moers defines in *Literary Women*. Panther Cañon is Thea's source of inspiration in Willa Cather's *The Song of the Lark*, just as other female sexual landscapes, such as Maggie's Red Deeps in George Eliot's *The Mill on the Floss*, are "evoked by women writers for the same purpose of solitary, feminine assertion" (259). Conversely, in the southern pastoral, the land is already too closely associated with female exploitation for women authors to reappropriate it as a positive *female* configuration. Scarlett's triumph is short-lived, then, because, never disassociated with "property" herself, she cannot continue to act as an independent agent amassing her own property.

The only way to present Scarlett's quest for identity and power is, literally, to make *her* "rape" the land, resulting in a continuation of a system that exploits human beings as capital. Employing "free" blacks and convicts on starvation wages at the sawmill is no better than keeping slaves on an antebellum plantation. Relying on Mammy and the other "darkies" to fulfill their same serving roles both before and after the war, Scarlett and the other whites, women and men, for all their nostalgia for the *lost* "old days," perpetuate their standards.

Given the accurate historical setting of the novel, one might argue that Scarlett has no other available means for managing her property. But Mitchell wrote *GWTW* in the 1920s and could have imagined more egalitarian relationships among the characters had she chosen to do so. *GWTW*'s ambivalence rests in its presentation of race more than gender. That it questions the available means for female autonomy and identity is clear. But, although Mitchell experiments with new roles for white women, she does not transfer this radical vision to black women characters.

After the war, Scarlett unofficially "inherits" Tara from her father and takes over his role as patriarchal head of the family. Ownership of property signals power, the only power recognizable in this society, so this transfer of control is a necessary step in Scarlett's quest for heroism. She extends her control over land—property—when she marries Frank Kennedy and begins building her sawmill enterprise in Atlanta. Her quest for power has now temporarily become male, both literally and figuratively. Atlanta society gossips and disapproves of a "lady" running a business— she has usurped her husband's role—and figuratively, the sawmills represent her possession of land, direct exploitation of its resources. She has, in a sense, "raped" the virgin forests in order to continue her climb to power.

Scarlett's desire to possess land and become a male hero is thwarted, however, by her conflicting needs for control and submission. While she is able to sidestep her traditional female role, she is nonetheless trapped by her gender and upbringing as a white southern lady. Ellen has trained her well to expect protection and direction from the white southern male. As much as she yearns for power and independence, she never outgrows her need to be controlled. Her periodic returns to Tara are provoked by a desire to be with her mother. Indeed, she associates the plantation with Ellen throughout the novel. Simultaneously, she wants to possess and be possessed by the land. "Mother" earth nurtures Scarlett. Her becoming nominal head of Tara is ironically as much a continuance of her worship of her mother and an emulation of her mother's position as an assumption of her father's role. Returning to Tara after the burning of Atlanta to find the house still standing but all the fields and surroundings ravaged, Scarlett feels betrayed both by her mother's death and by the land which can no longer provide sustenance. As Helen Irvin points out, Scarlett's incomplete gender role transformation is actually underlined by her dependence on Tara for continued nurturance (59). Her need for the land is paradoxical. While it provides sustenance and strength for her to face her problems, it also promotes a symbiotic relationship. The more it gives, the more it demands homage.

The two rape scenes confirm the protagonist's inability to claim the role of the male hero. Wherever traditional motifs surface in the novel, Scarlett's quest for female heroism is undermined. Rape or exploitation of the female body provides the basis of conflict in the southern pastoral. Ownership of woman is crucial in justifying control of property. Again, because the novel depends metaphorically upon the southern garden, structurally, it repeats the story of the Fall: land is violated through an assault on white womanhood.

The first assault, which occurs on Scarlett's way home from one of her sawmills, is "punishment" for her accumulation of property. Leslie Fiedler claims that this scene alters the stereotype of the black "beast" rapist by depicting two men, a white and black ("*GWTW*: The Feminization of the Anti-Tom Novel" 204–5). The black man, nonetheless, is Scarlett's main attacker. She *has* stolen the male script in this case by assuming financial support of her family and Tara. Ostensibly, her successful business embarrasses Atlanta society because she breaks the code of southern loyalty by doing business with the Yankees—and profiting hugely by it. But Rhett explains to her the underlying reasons why she is shunned:

> All you've done is to be different from other women and you've made a little success at it. As I've told you before, that is the one unforgivable sin in any society. Be different and be damned! Scarlett, the mere fact that you've made a success of your mill is an insult to every man who hasn't succeeded. Remember, a well-bred female's place is in the home and she should know nothing about this busy, brutal world. . . . (670)

The characters' hatred of the Yankees cloaks the novel's deep sexism and racism. Scarlett's actions threaten the very system of white supremacy, for not only does she nullify the role of the passive, helpless female who needs chivalrous, male protection, but as India Wilkes later tells her, ". . . you've ridden about the woods exposing yourself to attack, you've exposed every well-be-haved woman in town to attack by putting temptation in the ways of darkies and mean white trash . . ." (787). Like the now emancipated "darkies," Scarlett refuses to stay in her appropriated place—the home.

Only by upholding the white southern woman as "victim" of black violence can the southern society retain its hierarchy. In crusading against postbellum southern lynching practices in 1892, Ida B. Wells explained that "white men used their ownership of the body of the white females as a terrain on which to lynch the black male." As critic Hazel Carby observes, southerners appealed to northerners on the grounds that lynching was necessary for the "protection" of the white southern lady, but this plea was actually an effective means of disguising their real purpose of denying the black vote ("Ideologies of Black Folk" 269–70). This means of ensuring white supremacy also pitted white women against black, a further reason, I contend, that Mitchell's use of male pastoral conventions precludes any possibility of interracial female friendship.

In one of the novel's more melodramatic descriptions of the ills of Reconstruction, the narrator explains: ". . . these ignominies and dangers were as nothing compared with the peril of white women, many bereft by the war of male protection. . . . It was the large number of outrages on women and the ever-present fear for the safety of their wives and daughters that drove Southern men to cold and trembling fury and caused the Ku Klux Klan to spring up overnight" (647). In her correspondence, Mitchell justifies the Klan in a similar way: "Members of the Klan knew that if unscrupulous or ignorant people were permitted to hold office in the South the lives and property of Southerners would not be safe" (162). *GWTW's* Klan members are all appropriately upstanding citizens, men who resort to violence only when absolutely necessary.[9]

The novel conflates white racial fear with fear of women's emancipation in the character of Archie, Scarlett's erstwhile, ex-convict bodyguard who quits her employment shortly before she is attacked in the woods. At one point Archie tells Scarlett why he was convicted; he murdered his wife: "She was layin' with my brother. . . . I ain't sorry none that I kilt her. Loose women ought to be kilt. The law ain't got no right to put a man in jail for that but I was sont" (746). Later, however, Archie is released when the Confederates need more men to help with fighting Sherman's army—the warden agreed with him that wife-killing was not really a crime. Again, the Cause justifies bigotry; Archie is hired because he hates a Yankee only *more* "than a nigger or a woman" (747).

The central rape scene in the novel occurs when Rhett assaults Scarlett at home after Ashley's birthday party. It can be read as the linking of racial fear with misogyny. Ironically, it substitutes structurally for the black assault on white "property" or woman. As Joel Williamson observes, Rhett functions in this scene not just as "dark" villain but as a *black* man. Williamson explains that Mitchell wrote an earlier novella, "'Ropa Carmagin," that portrays the white heroine falling in love with a mulatto former slave. Mitchell's husband did not like the "theme" of miscegenation, however, and urged her to put it aside (102).

The violence of this scene is unmistakable. Seizing Scarlett and forcing her back to their marriage bed, Rhett becomes a "mad stranger" who carries her to a "black darkness she did not know, darker than death" (929). Scarlett's enjoyment of being subdued, the ecstasy of her surrender, is "primitive," and the resulting fetus can only be aborted as a product of a tabooed coupling. If she were to admit her enjoyment of sex to her husband, as indirectly she tries to the morning after the rape, the pastoral myth that the novel conforms to would be completely undermined, for repressed sexuality is what actually determines the place and role of the southern belle. Sex, and female sexuality, are forbidden in the novel because they would finally violate the virginal facade of the southern woman. Linked with miscegenation, female sexuality is doubly taboo. Consequently, the denial of sexuality in the novel indicates its ultimate conformity to the male pastoral mode.

Rhett's violent vengeance in this scene is not merely his jealousy of Ashley. After all, he tells Scarlett, ". . . I wouldn't have grudged him your body. I know how little bodies mean—especially women's bodies. But I do grudge him your heart and your dear, hard, unscrupulous, stubborn mind. . . . I can buy women cheap. But I do want your mind and your heart, and I'll never have them . . ." (928). The language of romance gives way to the text of male ownership—Rhett did buy Scarlett by marrying her, yet she continues to try to assert the right to own her body.

Furthermore, Scarlett attempts to steal the hero's role directly from him. Jan Cohn explains, "Yankee capitalism wins the war and brings a new economic system to the South. In this economic structure, Ashley as hero succumbs, giving way to Rhett, the new hero with the requisite vitality and aggressiveness to succeed" (148). Rhett had assumed that, once Scarlett married him, she would give up her capitalist scheming. Her refusal to give up the public for the domestic sphere afterwards conflicts directly with his plans to establish a bourgeois home. Cohn reads the ending of the novel—when Scarlett loses Rhett, the "hero"—as punishment "for her economic aggressiveness, her fiercely heroic but finally unwomanly determination never to go hungry again, and for her consequent failure to discover the true hero" (150). I argue that Scarlett's failure is not in identifying the true "hero," i.e., Rhett, but in not understanding how *she*, as much as all other forms of capital in the novel (land and black or convict labor), is valued as property. Like any other good businessman, when the investment is not profitable, Rhett cuts his losses.

Scarlett's relationships with other men in the novel who are not economic competitors are not as inherently conflicting as her relationship with Rhett. It is in these relationships that Mitchell begins to imagine new ways for men and women to interact. Although throughout most of the novel Scarlett pines for an Ashley that she doesn't really understand, in some ways he would be a better match for her than Rhett. Opposite temperaments often *do* make stronger couples for each would compensate for the other's weaknesses. Scarlett's headstrong nature would have been balanced by Ashley's reflectiveness. Ashley also lacks the chauvinism that would make him a domineering husband. Scarlett realizes *before* the climax of the novel that he is more companion than lover. The "scandal" that shames Scarlett at Ashley's birthday party is actually based upon this discovery of friendship: "The comfort of his arms helped dry her sudden tears. Ah, it was good to be in his arms, without passion, without tenseness, to be there as a loved friend. Only Ashley who shared her memories and her youth, who knew her beginnings and her present could understand" (915). From a starry-eyed sixteen year old, Scarlett has finally matured enough to see Ashley, not for the gallant gentleman he might have been in the old order, but for the broken but realistic man he has become.

Another male/female friendship often overlooked in the novel is between Scarlett and Will Benteen, the poor white ex-soldier Scarlett appoints to manage Tara. Not only does he listen to and advise her on plantation matters, he becomes everyone's confidant. A member of a lower class, he and his power are not threatening, and his role is usually considered a female one since it concerns private not public matters. Like Melanie, he demonstrates keen insight for character, understanding both Carreen's pining for her dead lover and Scarlett's ambition for power.

Scarlett and Will share a love for Tara that enables mutual respect. Their companionship is reminiscent of the bond Dorinda Oakley in Glasgow's *Barren Ground* establishes with her second husband, Nathan, when they work on the farm together. In one scene, Will admits to Scarlett: "I can't leave Tara. It's home to me, Scarlett, the only real home I ever knew and I love every stone of it. I've worked on it like it was mine. And when you put out work on somethin', you come to love it. You know what I mean?" Scarlett immediately understands, for she is equally devoted to Tara, and "her heart went out in a surge of warm affection for him, hearing him say he, too, loved the thing she loved best" (685). Affectionate and natural with him, Scarlett rests her head on his shoulder as they discuss plantation business riding home for her father's funeral.

Like Dorinda, however, Scarlett is able to maintain this kind of openness and honesty only when she is a class superior. Scarlett's and Will's alliance is made possible by their difference in social status. Were she to stay on Tara and farm the land with him, she could no longer be the white southern "lady" she aspires to be. In traditional southern pastoral, the "belle" can never marry below her class standing—romance and economic status are integrally linked. Scarlett is shocked to find out about her contemporaries who marry either Yankees or poor white overseers. Both the women and the land (former plantations) they represent are thus devalued, and Scarlett resists identifying with these women. Mitchell solves this postwar class dilemma by having the poor white Will marry Scarlett's stand-in, her sister Suellen. Significantly, the description of Tara after the war shows how the plantation has essentially been transformed into a yeoman farm:

> Scarlett's heart swelled with affection and gratitude to Will who
> had done all of this. Even her loyalty to Ashley could not make her
> believe he had been responsible for much of this well-being, for
> Tara's bloom was not the work of a planter-aristocrat, but of the
> plodding, tireless 'small farmer' who loved his land. It was a 'two-
> horse' farm, not the lordly plantation of other days with pastures
> stretching as far as eye could see. But what there was of it was
> good. . . . (695–96)

While the imagery of Tara changes, Scarlett's relationship to the land does not. Her determination to "hold" Tara even "if she had to break the back of every person on it" (428) represents her rigid attitude toward changing class interactions after the war; after all, it is not she, finally, who has to labor on the land. Her climb to power in Atlanta results not from meaningful work, like Dorinda's, but from her manipulation and exploitation of the labor of others. Scarlett finally preserves the hierarchical, racist system of the old order because, as "patriarch" of the plantation, it serves her well.

Her inability to form intimate, trusting relationships with most other women hinges upon an economic relationship to the land. Especially before the war, Scarlett views women as rivals rather than friends. When the O'Hara girls arrive at the Wilkes's barbecue in the opening scene, the narrator comments: "No girl in the County, with possible exception of the empty-headed Cathleen Culvert, really liked Scarlett" (88). She is more successful at flirting than they—and catching the "right" man is a desperate competition since this is the sole way of assuring financial stability. Courtship in antebellum southern society, as in Victorian Britain, is property negotiation. Jan Cohn discusses how marriages are arranged in the feudal society of the Old South. Because Ashley is to

inherit wealth—the plantation Twelve Oaks—"he can have economic aggressiveness without a display of threatening economic
energy. . . . [W]ith Scarlett, he is not the pursuer but the pursued"
(146–7). Scarlett's father, a shrewd businessman, realizes, however,
that the Wilkes's wealth is beyond his daughter's grasp. Trying to
discourage Scarlett from setting her heart on Ashley, Gerald
O'Hara encourages her to think about the Tarleton boys: "Think it
over, daughter. Marry one of the twins and then the plantations
will run together and Jim Tarleton and I will build you a fine
house, right where they join . . ." (36). Ashley will marry Melanie
because the Wilkes's family property must be preserved. He tells
Scarlett, "She is like me, part of my blood. . ." (119). In the
antebellum South of Mitchell's novel, blood more than romance
determines marriages.

In Atlanta, Scarlett meets disapproval even more with women
than with the men whose position she tries to usurp because she
threatens the economic system they live by. India Wilkes's insinuat-
ing remarks become direct insults the night of the sewing circle
when the southern men go out to avenge Scarlett's assault. She
accuses Scarlett of an absence of "good breeding" and tells her,
"You don't care about being protected! If you did you'd never
have exposed yourself as you have done all these months, prissing
yourself about this town, showing yourself off to strange men,
hoping they'll admire you! What happened to you this afternoon
was just what you deserved . . ." (786). Scarlett has broken the
southern code by attempting to act without the protection of her
menfolk. Belle Watling, especially, refuses to associate with Scarlett,
since Scarlett behaves neither like a "lady" of good breeding, nor a
prostitute, whose livelihood still depends upon men.

Soon, Scarlett begins to realize that only Mammy (who, nonetheless, continually criticizes Scarlett's shocking behavior) and
Melanie remain loyal to her. Melanie, in fact, as many critics have
commented, serves as foil and alter-ego for the protagonist. She
allows Scarlett to rebel from the conventional expectations of soci-

ety. As a kind of mother figure—the only intimate bond Scarlett can maintain with any woman—Melanie stands loyally by her and loves her no matter the cost, welcoming her into her home despite society's censure.

The friendship between Scarlett and Melanie represents perhaps the greatest departure from traditional southern pastoral in the novel. In male versions of the pastoral, bonding between women would digress too much from the romantic plot. Although Scarlett remains unconscious of their mutual dependency until the end, she and Melanie work and live side by side from the day their husbands depart for the war. Melanie rescues Scarlett from social isolation while Scarlett provides economic sustenance and physical endurance for the Wilkeses. She also saves Melanie and her baby during the siege of Atlanta.

One scene that demonstrates their mutuality occurs at Tara after the war when a Yankee soldier arrives to plunder the plantation. Scarlett arms herself with a rifle, and simultaneously Melanie grabs a saber. After she shoots, Scarlett looks up and their eyes meet. "'Why—why—she's like me!'" she thinks, and "[w]ith a thrill she looked up at the frail swaying girl for whom she had never had any feelings but of dislike and contempt. Now, struggling against hatred for Ashley's wife, there surged a feeling of admiration and comradeship . . ." (434).

Another moment like this occurs when the two run to put out a fire the Union soldiers set in Tara's kitchen. After Melanie saves Scarlett from being engulfed by flames by throwing a rug over her, Scarlett again admits her tender feelings for her: ". . . she was too tired to struggle, because the words of praise brought balm to her spirit and because, in the dark smoke-filled kitchen, there had been born a greater respect for her . . . a closer feeling of comradeship" (463). But this kind of teamwork stops when they move back to Atlanta. It seems that Scarlett can only recognize the value of female friendship during moments of great danger like these while the men are away at war.

The climax of the novel occurs at Melanie's deathbed where Scarlett finally realizes that she is losing her closest friend. Significantly, she links Melanie in her memory with her own mother:

> Yes, Melanie had been there that day with a sword in her small hand, ready to do battle for her. And now, as Scarlett looked sadly back, she realized that Melanie had always been there beside her with a sword in her hand, unobtrusive as her own shadow, loving her, fighting for her with blind passionate loyalty. . . . Scarlett felt her courage and self-confidence ooze from her as she realized that the sword which had flashed between her and the world was sheathed forever. . . . Suddenly it was as if Ellen were lying behind that closed door, leaving the world for a second time. Suddenly she was standing at Tara again with the world about her ears. . . . (1000)

This poignant realization of love is deeper, more meaningful than Scarlett's desperate recognition of her passion for Rhett. The bond the two women establish moves beyond the economic rivalry of the prewar society.

Aside from Melanie, the only other woman character in the novel that Scarlett trusts is Mammy. Again, intimacy is only possible because their relationship is based on the mother/child interaction. Like a spoiled child, Scarlett orders Mammy about even after she assumes the adult management of Tara. Scarlett's periodic rebellions against convention—ruining her delicate white hands, attempting to travel to Atlanta by herself—are met with stubborn insistence that she behave. Mammy alternately scolds and supports her. It is to her bosom that Scarlett runs after Rhett leaves her for the last time, because as she realizes, Mammy, more than anyone else, maintains the old ways. As we will see in chapter 3 with Willa Cather's character Till, the mammy, even more than the plantation mistress, often becomes representative of the old order through carrying out its social prescriptions.

But Mammy's depiction in the novel is paradoxical, at once symbolic of white respectability and class, and, as the most detailed portrait of a "darky," representative of the lower status—or actually nonpersonhood—of black characters. The narrator introduces her in the first scene:

> Mammy emerged from the hall, a huge old woman with the small, shrewd eyes of an elephant. She was shining black, pure African, devoted to her last drop of blood to the O'Haras, Ellen's mainstay. . . . Mammy was black, but her code of conduct and her sense of pride were as high as or higher than those of her owners. She had been raised in the bedroom of Solange Robillard, Ellen O'Hara's mother, a dainty, cold high-nosed Frenchwoman, who spared neither her children nor her servants their just punishment for any infringement of decorum. . . . (25)

The transfer of Mammy from the Robillard to the O'Hara household certifies Gerald's class ascendance. At the same time, however, as "a huge old woman with the small, shrewd eyes of an elephant," Mammy appears grotesque, almost as animal-like as the "black apes" the narrator describes who live in Atlanta's shanty town. Like the inclusion of the Klan and lynching, the dehumanization of black characters in the novel, Hazel Carby claims, encodes white fear of black urban migration in the 1920s and 1930s (*Reconstructing Womanhood* 130–31). Mammy's presence offers a solution to this potentially threatening movement; like the other faithful servants in *GWTW*, she scorns freedom and accepts white supremacy as a "civilized" system.

Scarlett's longing for Mammy in the closing scene parallels her need for her mother. As we will see in *Dessa Rose,* for the protagonist Rufel, the black mammy is often appropriated as substitute mother. In *GWTW,* Mammy and Tara are conflated at the end of the novel as Scarlett's primal mother, enduring, unchanging, demanding, but always forgiving:

> She stood for a moment remembering small things, the avenue of dark cedars leading to Tara, the banks of cape jessamine bushes, vivid green against the white walls, the fluttering white curtains.

And Mammy would be there. Suddenly she wanted Mammy
desperately, as she had wanted her when she was a little girl,
wanted the broad bosom on which to lay her head, the gnarled
black hand on her hair. Mammy, the last link with the old days.
(1024)

Scarlett's yearning for a black mother in this scene links her
with the southern white male protagonist. Like a male hero, the
female substitution still attempts to "possess" the land. As a disembodied earth mother, Mammy has finally displaced the role of the
white southern lady as representative of the southern garden.
However, the garden is evoked here not as landscape but as the
plantation house itself, the last vestige of the old order. Like
Faulkner's Dilsey, Mammy never questions her role as protectress
of the South's race and class hierarchy; rather than developed
characters, both become emblems of the *new* Old South.

By switching gender roles in her novel, Mitchell creates a
possibility for a change in the pastoral tradition. She imagines a
female hero who, freed from the romantic plot, can act autono-
mously. Significantly, like Ellen Glasgow's and Willa Cather's female protagonists, Scarlett derives strength from her relationship
to the land. Another element of female pastoral explored in *GWTW*
is friendship between women, particularly that between Scarlett
and Melanie.

Yet the author never changes the traditional representation of
the landscape as female, so ultimately Scarlett's return to Tara
indicates her entrapment in the southern garden. Since Mammy
and Tara are conflated at the end of *GWTW*, Scarlett becomes
earth's daughter. Figuratively, she receives nurturance from the
"beautiful red earth" of the plantation.

Mitchell's use of imagery to describe Scarlett's return to Tara
in the closing scene is telling: "She had gone back to Tara once in
fear and defeat and she had emerged from its sheltering walls
strong and armed for victory. What she had done once, somehow—please God, she could do again!" (1023). Scarlett views her

experiences in the public world as a conflict for power and dominance. She appropriates typically patriarchal methods and attitudes here. Tara is not a private place for reflection and rejuvenation but a shelter or a fort from which the "hero" can emerge victorious. The point is not that Scarlett should avoid the struggle for power but that she will go to any lengths to achieve it. Like Rhett and Grandma Fontaine, Scarlett is "buckwheat." She learns to "play along with lesser folks and . . . take what she can get from them" (709) rather than work cooperatively with the rest of the community.

GWTW does invert the structure and characters of the plantation novel. But this experiment in gender never completely achieves the definition of a new kind of pastoral, an alternative vision to the version of twentieth-century male writers. Both inscribe fear of a changing order. The Civil War is a stand-in for the social turbulence surrounding World War I. As much as the novel expresses Scarlett's emancipation from the role of white southern lady, it suppresses and contains her rebellion from the code of white supremacy. Too much independent action would threaten the institutions created to preserve race, class, and sex hierarchy. What the novel finally demonstrates is that, for Mitchell at least, feminist fantasy could not work in a masculinist form. The pastoral must undergo a more radical revision in order to envision a form of female empowerment that not only liberates the protagonist but changes the oppressive system under which she lives. In Willa Cather's last novel, *Sapphira and the Slave Girl* (1940), we see the beginnings of this change through its vision of female community.

3. Willa Cather's Ironic Plantation "Romance": *Sapphira and the Slave Girl*

The history of every country begins in the heart of a man
or a woman.
— *O Pioneers!*

She would go up out of Egypt to a better land . . . to make
her own way in this world where nobody is altogether free, and
the best that can happen to you is to walk your own way and be
responsible to God only. Sapphira's darkies were better cared
for, better fed and better clothed, than the poor whites in the
mountains. Yet what ragged, shag-haired, squirrel shooting
mountain man would change places with Sampson, his trusted
head miller?
— *Sapphira and The Slave Girl*

Willa Cather's last novel, *Sapphira and the Slave Girl* (1940), seems
hardly an appropriate study in the development of a female pastoral tradition. It is clearly not the kind of celebratory pastoral that
Cather writes about midwestern farm life.[1] In her biography *Willa
Cather: The Emerging Voice*, Sharon O'Brien demonstrates how
Cather was able to develop her mature fiction after escaping her
mother and her southern heritage. Living and writing in the Mid-
west allowed Cather to create an imaginative response to an
"unclaimed" landscape. But in this final pastoral, the author returns to her Virginia heritage in order to depict the treacherous
underside of the antebellum planter society. *Sapphira* undermines
the mythic construction of the *southern* garden. Unlike Ellen
Glasgow, who focuses on yeoman farmers in her later pastorals,

and Margaret Mitchell, whose *Gone with the Wind* can be seen as "romantic racism," Cather makes race the crux of her characters' inner conflicts.[2] She takes the dismantling of the patriarchal southern pastoral one step further than Mitchell by exposing the falsity of the naturalized female character—emphasizing how woman is linked to landscape only in male characters' eyes. Romance is no longer even the ostensible plot complication. Also, at the end of the novel, we are given a picture of female community that suggests an alternative to patriarchal control.

This is not to claim that the novel re-imagines the southern garden without oppression. Because *Sapphira and the Slave Girl* depicts plantation instead of farm life, like *Gone with the Wind*, it ultimately precludes female autonomy and the development of cooperative communities. Plantations were structured as hierarchical, oppressive systems. Cather's pastoral is further compromised by the author's ambivalence about its autobiographical elements. Based at least partly upon Cather's great-grandmother, the female protagonist Sapphira is alternately pictured as admirable and self-serving. A degree of nostalgia overshadows the narrative, making it even more difficult to discern the author's irony.

As in *Gone with the Wind*, the plot focuses upon the drive for power and how women—in this case Sapphira—are able to grasp and maintain it. Yet Cather's novel *begins* where Mitchell's ends: Sapphira is a less appealing character than Scarlett because her drive for power results in the objectification and victimization of her slave Nancy. Despite the almost pleasant description of plantation ritual and order, the novel creates an atmosphere of guilt and, as Cather told Edith Lewis, suggests more by what it omits rather than what is specifically narrated (183). We discover Sapphira's design to victimize Nancy through innuendo, not admission. Sapphira and Henry always use "Bluebell," another young slave woman who is not as responsible about her duties, as a sort of code word whenever they discuss Nancy's fate. Finally, the author implicates herself in this racist, oppressive system in the epilogue by shifting the viewpoint to the first person. Eugénie Hamner explains how the five-year-old child narrator represents Cather herself (348). In this novel, unlike any of the other pastorals discussed thus far, white women cannot escape the responsibility they bear for the sexual victimization of their black counterparts.

Instead of creating a new type of woman-centered plot, as she does in her earlier novels, the author sets up and disappoints expectations for readers already familiar with the plantation novel. Merrill Skaggs asserts that Cather mocks the conventions of this genre in order to experiment with a new form of narrative (3). The opening scene, in which Sapphira discusses with her husband the possibility of selling Nancy, is perhaps an intentional ironic allusion to the beginning of Harriet Beecher Stowe's *Uncle Tom's Cabin* where it is Mr. Shelby who wants to sell his slaves and his wife who resists. Not an openly polemical novel like Stowe's, neither is it merely a nostalgic recollection of manners as biographers Brown (311) and Woodress (263) insist. Although Deborah Carlin believes the novel's problematic narrative form undercuts the evils of slavery depicted, I believe rather that Cather creates an equivocating portrayal of antebellum life in order to invite readers to judge for themselves.

The irony of this plantation "romance" is established early. The setting resembles that of *The Professor's House* (1925) more than that of Cather's other "land" novels, centering on interiors rather than exteriors. Sapphira's ritualistic teas, Henry's room at the mill, and Nancy's pallet in the hall outside her mistress' room comprise the main scenes. Rather than linger over a description of the lavish Mill House, the narrator gives a brief summary of its style "well known to all Virginians" and then proceeds to detail what lies behind its trimmed hedges: "another world; a helter-skelter scattering, like a small village . . ." (20). The reader is shown the plantation world from "behind the scenes": we are given the black perspective of the white system. Indeed, the author later wrote that she began the novel with "a memory of Negro voices."[3] And the significant action of the plot, Martin's attempted rape of Nancy, occurs in this hidden netherworld. No one understands or responds to the threat posed to Nancy in this instance. Only when Nancy directly appeals to Sapphira's daughter, Rachel Blake, do any whites attempt to interfere in the assault, even though Henry has been vaguely aware of the problem all along.

This shift in narrative focus from the white to the black story signals a reversal of interest in the pastoral plot itself. Instead of the white woman as the seduced, innocent victim, we have Nancy Till, the young "slave girl," who fights off the degenerate white Martin Colbert. Cather's plantation world reveals the reality behind the southern myth encoded in popular novels like *Gone with the Wind*. It is, after all, the black woman who was most vulnerable to sexual victimization. Nell Painter explains the relations among class, gender, and race in antebellum society, analyzing how black women slaves began to be victimized: "That particular groups of women have been seen as outside the moral system of others has long provided men an excuse for rape. During the last two millennia, men have turned the vulnerability to sexual assault of groups of women into a reputation for sensuality" (58). In *Sapphira*, Cather refutes the stereotype of the black earth mother or "whore" that developed from this association of female slaves with unbridled sexuality.

Male slaves were also misrepresented by southern myth as sex fiends. Their supposed assault on white womanhood became an excuse for lynching—in actuality, an effective means of enforcing white supremacy. Twentieth-century white male versions of the pastoral confirm this myth of the black rapist whether in ante- or postbellum narratives; Tate's *The Fathers* and Faulkner's *Light in August* are only two examples. Again, Cather's novel refutes southern plantation myth by inverting such character types. Her antebellum romance focuses on the assault of a *black* woman by a *white* man.

In addition to recasting the victims of violence in southern myth, Cather also revises gender roles. Minrose Gwin argues that, as Nancy's rescuer, Rachel Blake functions both as the representative of the new order (the rebellious "son") and as the novel's white "mammy" (144). Sapphira, paradoxically, is the representation of patriarchal power. Her ability to determine others' lives identifies her with the oppressive system. Henry Colbert, her husband, is a kind of "feminized" bystander. He takes the role usually reserved for the white plantation mistress who can (or will) do nothing to thwart her husband's control. Till, Nancy's mother, and more important, Sapphira's loyal servant, becomes an emblem of the aristocratic order where appearances and ritual are more important than personhood. We do not admire her loyalty the way we do Mitchell's Mammy in *Gone with the Wind*. In *GWTW*, Mammy's family is essentially white; the kinship of the black characters is de-emphasized. But in Cather's novel Till's betrayal of her own daughter is all too apparent.

Finally, having inverted the standard stereotypes of the plantation romance, Cather questions the source of the evil invading the southern garden. As Marilyn Arnold points out, it is the southern system of order and manners itself that enslaves both master and chattel (325). Sapphira is controlled by this system as much as Nancy, for she is constrained to follow certain rituals in order to maintain her power. She proceeds by indirect and insidious means to assert her will. When Henry refuses to consider selling any slaves, including Nancy, she plots her slave's ruin by secretly writing a letter to his nephew Martin, a well known rake. She cannot order Nancy's removal from the plantation and from serving her husband without violating propriety, so she must thwart Henry's nominal authority through cunning.

It is this determination to attain power and property at any cost that eventually overwhelms Sapphira's humanity; she is not inhumane to begin with. Her daughter Rachel remembers several incidences when she was extremely generous to her slaves, for instance when she tries to buy a wife for the lovesick Tansy Dave

and continues to provide for him even when his madness prohibits
him from working. Sapphira's sympathy for old Jezebel, in fact,
seems to stem from a genuine respect for the other's faithful labor.
As Sapphira remembers, the two worked side by side on the plantation for many years:

> When I sit out on the porch on a day like this, and look around, I
> often think how we used to get up and rake over the new flower-
> beds and transplant before it got hot. And you used to run down to
> the creek and break off alder branches, and stick them all around
> the plants we'd set out, to keep the sun off. I expect you remember
> those things, too. . . (87–88)

Lest we begin to condone Sapphira's participation in the system,
immediately after the touching scene of Sapphira's visit to Jezebel,
the narrator takes us back to the slave woman's past and recounts
her harrowing journey on a slave ship across the Atlantic Ocean.
Again, the picture of Sapphira's involvement in slavery is somewhat softened. She is only one in a succession of other masters.
Still, the narrator never comments on or excuses Sapphira's actions
despite her fair or kind treatment of her own slaves.

By taking a patriarchal position of control, Sapphira inadvertently adopts a male view, just as her husband Henry, choosing to
remain on the sidelines, shirks responsibility for his part in Nancy's
victimization by playing the female role of submission and passivity. Sapphira becomes like certain other Cather male protagonists.
She views women reductively. Although the author had abandoned
the "pastoral impulse" years earlier, her pastoral novels show male
characters still responding to women as landscape. Nancy is to
Sapphira what Antonia is to Jim Burden. Both represent a mythic
construct of "natural" sexuality, but Sapphira perceives Nancy as a
threat instead of as an embodiment of a dream as Jim does
Antonia.

Though Cather's natural imagery is more subtle in this novel
than in her earlier works, the male view of femininity is repre-

sented when Martin Colbert tries to seduce Nancy while she is picking cherries. This "garden" scene is like Emil and Marie's orchard in *O Pioneers!* which, according to Jennifer Bailey, symbolizes the corruption "in that very arena where conventional versions find ennobling fulfillment" (399). In both cases, the enclosed space signals danger for the female character, contrasting with the open fields where Alexandra and Glasgow's Dorinda find freedom.

When Martin first arrives at the cherry trees, he "hadn't meant to do more than tease" Nancy (182), yet overcome by her beauty and the lovely scent of the cherry trees, he "stepped lightly on the chair, caught [Nancy's] bare ankles, and drew her two legs about his cheeks like a frame" (180). In a few words, Cather conveys the real danger of Nancy's attraction for Martin. He is not titillated by flirtation or even her alluring presence but by associating her with nature. Martin *will* see Nancy as a natural sex object no matter what attempts she makes to dispel this view. Instead of representing the order of society and beauty of southern womanhood as in the typical plantation romance, Cather's southern garden invokes the "original sin" of a culture that exploits human flesh.[4]

The male objectification and appropriation of female sexuality in *Sapphira*—as in *O Pioneers!*—invites tragedy. Were it not for Rachel's interference, Nancy would have been raped, for Henry fails to act against his nephew. He views the young woman in a different but equally reductive light. To Henry, Nancy represents that pure, inspiring influence that the white southern heroine usually holds. Alone in his mill room reading *Pilgrim's Progress*, he sees "Nancy's face and figure plain in Mercy" (67), and when this view of her is threatened by Sampson's report of Martin's misconduct, the miller feels "strongly disinclined" to see her since "it would not be the same as yesterday. Something disturbing had come between them since then" (192).

That something is, of course, the recognition that Nancy is a flesh-and-blood woman after all, a fact that Henry tries diligently to avoid until Rachel confronts him with it directly. Later, consider-

ing how he might "buy off" Martin in order to save Nancy, the
miller feels a sudden empathy for his nephew: "The Colbert in
him threatened to raise its head after long hibernation" (209).
Even the thoughtful, kind, "feminized" master is susceptible to the
view of the black woman as readily available for male sexual gratification.

Illicit sex thus becomes the central focus of Cather's last pastoral. In the beginning of her writing career, Cather had to separate
her female "victims" from her female heroes in order to change
the destiny of her protagonists. Edith Lewis explains these different
characterizations in Cather's early short fiction: "The Bohemian
Girl" and then "Alexandra" characterize two different creative im-
pulses (83). In the first story, passion is represented typically in the
romantic plot. The heroine fulfills her destiny when she escapes
with her lover (who, though male, is identified more closely with
the narrative voice). In the second story, from which she developed
O Pioneers!, Cather depicts the protagonist's passion in the relationship to the land itself and allows the female hero autonomy. *O
Pioneers!* combines the two plots, the conventional and unconventional, subsuming the first into a commentary on Alexandra's
emotional development.

But the two strands of female development in Cather's fiction
are never wholly combined. As in Ellen Glasgow's *Barren Ground*
and *Vein of Iron*, the sexually passionate woman often continues to
"pay the price" for engaging in conventional romantic relationships while the artist/pioneer woman for whom Alexandra becomes the prototype—finds contentment through individual triumph. In *My Antonia* (1918), Antonia Shimerda represents the
latter kind of female protagonist: Jim Burden strips her of threatening sexuality by reducing her to an earth mother stereotype.
Lena, by contrast, the alluring city girl, never achieves a recognized place in her hometown community—or in Burden's narrative. Marian Forrester, the female protagonist in Cather's *A Lost
Lady* (1923), is more willful and independent than either Lena or

Antonia yet she still directs her energies toward male-female romance. Her passion—or creativity—remains constrained within
the patriarchal culture, just as the narrator, Niel Herbert, a resur-
rected Jim Burden figure, tries to constrain her within the bounds
of his Victorian propriety.

Only when the female protagonist rejects the male gaze and
avoids the trap of male betrayal does she achieve complete autonomy—and a voice in the narrative. Cather's novels, in this
sense, contain experiments with female development and plot
which move further and further from the conventional romance,
the final result being a novel which, according to Edith Lewis, is
"without a heroine—the central figure is a cold and rather repel-
lent character" (185). Sapphira, to many critics, is a protagonist so
willful and domineering that she calls into question the female
quest for power and autonomy.

The reader encounters her, not, as with Cather's earlier female protagonists, as a headstrong young woman, but rather as an
aging matriarch. Like Katherine Anne Porter's and William
Faulkner's grandmother figures, Sapphira achieves her authority
through her role as family elder and property owner. Significantly,
Porter and Faulkner are able to depict female authority only by
absenting the older male. The grandmothers in Porter's *Flowering
Judas* (1930), in the group of Miranda stories in "The Old Order,"
and in Faulkner's *The Unvanquished* (1938) are widows—they rule
over sons, not husbands. Cather's grandmother is perhaps "repel-
lent" because she seizes control laterally instead of, like Porter's
Granny Weatherall, waiting for the role.

The portrait of Sapphira, however, cannot be regarded merely
as the end of a spectrum of stronger and stronger Cather female
heroes; this view accounts for only part of her character. She is also
represented, ironically, as a white southern lady, though of a different stamp from that of the pastoral-romance prototype. On the
surface she resembles Mrs. Templeton in "Old Mrs. Harris"[5] and
Marian Forrester in her concern for appearances and ritual. Again,

the narrator's view of Sapphira is ambivalent, vacillating between revealing Sapphira's overfastidiousness and need for control and admiring her ability to keep order and grace in the household and direct plantation business.

This shifting viewpoint is especially noticeable if one examines descriptions of the matriarch in Books I and VIII. In the first half of the novel, the irony is much sharper. We see Sapphira at her desk, "in her morning jacket and capon . . . writing a letter. She wrote with pause for deliberation, which was unusual. She was not unhandy with the pen. . . This morning she was composing a letter to a nephew—a letter of invitation. It was meant to be cordial, but not too cordial. . . ." (30). Sapphira's neat hand and obvious self-assurance are undercut by the intention of her action; with one simple letter she sets in motion her plan to ruin Nancy.

As the plot progresses in the early chapters of the novel, the narrator becomes even more critical of Sapphira's role as plantation mistress. The concept of the "lady" that Cather only gently mocks in *A Lost Lady* provides a central focus for irony. The reader witnesses the danger in the power of sexual attractiveness, traditionally the main source of a southern belle's control. Marian Forrester, the earlier protagonist, begins to lose power when she is no longer sexually alluring to men. Sapphira maintains power, conversely, through managing and redirecting sex between others: she marries Till off to Jeff, "the capon man" (43), in order to keep her slave continually under her own sphere of influence, and she denies or prevents a friendship between Henry and Nancy by introducing the threat of sexual attraction. As in Glasgow's fiction, the primary sexual battle of Cather's southern pastoral—conflict between male and female protagonists—is deflected. But, while Glasgow uses landscape imagery to represent the negotiation of sexual passion, Cather introduces the black slave woman as pawn. Sapphira avoids making her own body sexually available and vulnerable by controlling the sexual availability of others—specifically, in this case, that of her slave Nancy.

Another characteristic of white "ladyhood" that Sapphira embodies and Cather subtly criticizes is her aristocratic pedigree. Accustomed to riding through Back Creek with the Dodderidge coat of arms on her carriage (35), Sapphira uses her rank to the fullest advantage. Though she marries beneath her status and shocks "the family friends" who "were more astonished than if she had declared her intention of marrying the gardener" (25), she also ensures her continued dominance over the family plantation. She resembles Scarlett O'Hara's mother, who uses class standing to assert her authority at Tara. Unlike Mrs. O'Hara, though, Sapphira actually owns the property she manages. Her husband Henry also prefers this matriarchal arrangement, as he tells her: "You're the master here, and I'm the miller. And that's how I like it to be" (50). In this regard, Sapphira's kind treatment of her servants can be seen as "noblesse oblige" rather than genuine humanity. Almost every action she takes has a purpose: to confirm and assert her authority.

The final characteristic of white southern womanhood that Cather criticizes through her portrait of Sapphira is selfishness. A true narcissist, Sapphira "thought of other people only in relation to herself" (220), a tendency that finally strips her of the ability to empathize with others, particularly Nancy or Rachel. Sapphira confuses egoism with self-sufficiency. Despairing when her growing invalidism prevents her from running the plantation completely independently, she thinks of her father and wishes "she had been kinder to him in the years when he was crippled and often in pain" (104). Still, this regret is cheap since she is not required to act on it. She cannot recognize the affinity she shares with her slaves, and yet, fearing that affinity, as her powerlessness grows and she becomes more dependent on her slaves' help, she sympathizes with them less.

Those who use and abuse others to obtain power can never be heroes in Cather's world. Sapphira's fate shows what happens when the desire for autonomy goes awry because of a fear of dependency. Sapphira is even reluctant to accept help or advice from her own family. She wants neither her husband nor her daughter to interfere in her command of the household. Rachel is scolded for entering her mother's chambers without express permission (13), and Henry must be specifically requested in order to appear for afternoon tea (49). The author suggests that her fear of dependency may go even deeper to a dread of intimacy, including sexuality, which is another determining factor in her cruel treatment of Nancy. Sapphira perceives all sexuality as a threat. Unlike Cather's earlier independent female heroes like Alexandra and Thea in *Song of the Lark*, she does not recognize how to channel her passion—or sexual energy—in a positive way. Finally, though potentially a great matriarch and ostensibly a great lady, she is represented as grotesque: her dropsy makes her appear pale and bloated until, as Susan Rosowski notes, she "illustrates the horror of an alienated life of empty forms" ("Willa Cather's American Gothic" 225).

Nonetheless, this harsh view of Sapphira's will for power is mediated in Book VIII when we witness the protagonist's death. After a prolonged estrangement from Rachel, Sapphira decides to forgive her daughter for helping Nancy escape with a simple but meaningful gesture of hospitality. She tells Henry, "Why not ask them to come spend the winter here with us? I would like to have them on my own account. . . . Rachel is very proud, but I expect if you told her I have failed, and we ought to have someone here, she would come" (267). Despite her emphasis on companionship for herself, Sapphira appears to be thinking about her granddaughter's and daughter's welfare here. She realizes that unless Rachel feels needed she will not come.

Henry also catches her intimation of her own forthcoming death, and the tender scene that follows seems to mitigate Sapphira's earlier uncompromising gestures:

Colbert felt a chill run through him. Sapphira had never before spoken to him of the possibility that something might happen to her this winter. Though now she mentioned this very casually, it struck terror to his heart. He seemed in a moment to feel sharply so many things he had grown used to and taken for granted: her long illness, with all its discomforts, and the intrepid courage with which she had faced the inevitable. He reached out for her two hands and buried his face in her palm. She felt his tears wet on her skin. For a long while he crouched thus, leaning against her chair, his head on her knee. (267)

Throughout the novel, the narrator creates these momentary portraits that so clearly reveal the nature of the characters' relationships. Sapphira is "mammy" to Henry in a kind of strange, ironic Madonna scene. The portrait simultaneously highlights and undercuts the understanding between wife and husband. A visual moment substitutes for a true resolution of conflict. This scene might be compared with Dorinda's and Nathan's moment of silent communion watching the stars after Dorinda has purchased Jason's property in *Barren Ground*. Both Cather and Glasgow imagine new ways for men and women to interact as friends and lovers, but each also fails to represent these relationships outside of such static moments.

But although of all her novels the last portrays the most willful abuse of others, it also depicts some of the most courageous and generous acts. Sapphira's calculated cruelty often draws the reader's attention away from Rachel, whose character combines the best of her parents' traits: she exhibits Henry's sensitivity and her mother's determination. Her assistance to Nancy in escaping Back Creek is motivated by a genuine desire to ensure the young woman's safety, not out of a sense of maternal control as is often the case in slave narratives. She fits Cather's definition of a pioneer better than her mother does.[6] In contrast to Henry, she is not afraid to risk Sapphira's disapproval or the consequences of breaking the law by helping a fugitive, and unlike her mother, she believes in a society without slavery and is willing to interact with

others on an equal rather than a hierarchical basis. Her tendency
to ignore social customs is prefigured early in the novel when
Sapphira reflects that her daughter "had always been difficult,—
rebellious toward the fixed ways which satisfied other folk" (15),
contrary to Sapphira's own overestimation of convention and authority.

Rachel's generosity toward others (she often goes out to nurse
her neighbors) underlines the speciousness of Sapphira's kindness, which is performed out of a sense of propriety:

> As she drove along, Mrs. Colbert was thinking it was fortunate that
> for once her daughter had been called to nurse in a prosperous
> family like the Thatchers. . . . Usually she was called out to some
> bare mountain cabin where she got nothing but thanks, and likely
> as not had to take along milk and eggs and her own sheets for the
> poor creature who was sick. Rachel was poor, and it was not much
> use to give her things. Whatever she had she took where it was
> needed most; and Mrs. Colbert certainly didn't intend to keep the
> whole mountain. (38)

Not intending "to keep the whole mountain" encapsulates Sapphira's attitude toward her neighbors. She is beholden to them
only as custom dictates, whereas Rachel, who believes funda-
mentally that the relationship of *owning* others is wrong (137), responds both to the call for help and to others' offer of assistance.
In fact, by rejecting her mother's model of complete—and dangerous—self-sufficiency, Rachel learns the values of community that
Cather extols in all her fiction. Leaving her mother's house and
rejecting her authority, she escapes the patriarchal impulse to
amass property, whether as land or as human beings.

In addition to providing an essential contrast to Sapphira's
egoism, Rachel's presence in the novel also serves as a link between the white and black worlds. Literally, she is Nancy's guide to
freedom, and figuratively she shares an affinity with the young
slave woman that suggests a possible healing from the wounds of

racism. As Nancy's "white mother" she teaches her self-respect without arrogance and offers a generous, loyal spirit for her to follow.

Just as Till is more obedient to Sapphira than loyal to her own daughter, so Rachel is more faithful to Nancy than she is to Sapphira. Each becomes an outcast as a result of this interracial bonding. Moreover, Rachel and Nancy are both potential victims of male exploitation. Although Rachel's "service" to her husband should in no way be compared to the dehumanization Nancy suffers in slavery, the two women both demonstrate a tendency to want to please others—they have been socialized to accept passive roles. Married young, Rachel devotes herself to serving her husband, preparing elaborate dinners for his important visitors but remaining in the kitchen during the meal (140). Nancy mimics this devotion in her attentive housekeeping of Henry's room at the mill.

The imagery in the novel confirms their susceptibility to the view of womanhood as self-sacrificing. Rachel and Nancy are the only characters who appreciate natural scenery. Each stops at significant moments to admire her beautiful surroundings. Both are associated with flowers, a sure sign of an idealized female character. Rachel's future husband "found her in the flower garden, separating tufts of clove pinks" (132), and Nancy gathers smokepipes to put in her beloved miller's room. Both fit the narrator's definition of the "will to self-abnegation" which "took the form of untiring service to a man's pleasure" (141), and it is clear from the plot that they are saved from this fate only by circumstance: Rachel's husband dies and Nancy is forced to leave the mill. These "disasters" are fortuitous for the two women, allowing each to develop her autonomy while maintaining a generous spirit toward others.

In the last book of the novel, Cather reinforces this nascent interracial friendship between women while confirming her vision of interdependent communities. Nancy's return to Back Creek

twenty-five years later echoes Rachel's previous homecoming after
her husband's death. In the first instance, Sapphira welcomes her
daughter from whom she had grown estranged, while in the second it is the daughter who must learn a new understanding in
order to forgive:

> Till had already risen; when the stranger followed my mother
> into the room, she . . . fell meekly into the arms of a tall, gold-
> skinned woman, who drew the little old darky to her breast and
> held her there, bending her face down over the head scantily
> covered with grey wool. Neither spoke a word. There was
> something Scriptural in that meeting, like the pictures in our old
> Bible. (283).

Embracing Till, Nancy forgives her for failing to protect her from
her white oppressor, and perhaps now recognizes her mother's
psychological as well as physical enslavement. Here the narrative
freezes for a brief moment to frame another "portrait" scene.
Cather introduces visual frames to close the gap between speech
and action. Yet, like the earlier Madonna image of Sapphira com-
forting Henry, this reconciliation is tinged with irony. Understanding between the two women is more symbolic than verbal. Language fails at significant moments in the plot when past betrayal is
revealed.

This scene can be compared to an earlier nonverbal gesture in
the novel—the miller's financial assistance to Nancy and Rachel
when Nancy flees the plantation. When Rachel approaches him to
ask for money, he replies, "Hush, Rachel, not another word! You
and me can't talk about such things . . ."(227). That night he
leaves the money in the pocket of his coat and hangs it by the
open window. The silence in this scene not only signifies the necessary avoidance of Sapphira but also underlines Henry's passivity.
Like Till, he is unable to give outright assistance to Nancy. Gesture
must compensate for spoken loyalty or reconciliation.

By returning to visit with Rachel and Rachel's daughter at the end of the novel, Nancy also crosses over the boundaries of separation between white and black women. Her return allows reconciliation among the characters and enables the reader to recognize her as an autonomous character, not merely an instrument of the plot. The seduced victim has become an empowered woman who presents herself without narrative interference since the narrator here is a nonjudgmental child. How different the journey is here than at the end of *My Antonia* where Jim Burden has to force-fit Antonia into his romantic vision.

In this instance, Nancy's and the author's return to Virginia are joined. By recreating Nancy's reunion with Till, Cather makes a pictorial completion of the bonding that the plot cannot quite accomplish. Perhaps this tender moment of embrace represents Cather's forgiveness of the sins of her own past as well as of Nancy's. After all, as Lewis reports, Cather wrote *Sapphira* out of affection for her parents and at the particular request of her father (182). Just as the novel is not merely sweet nostalgia, it is also not simply condemnation of an evil system.

The narrative itself never judges Sapphira, but neither does it forgive her previous actions at her death. Many critics see this aspect of the novel as problematic. In fact, the narrator's sympathy for Sapphira never overwhelms the dark picture of her exploitation of others in order to gain power. Sapphira is clearly *not* an admirable character. But, like all of Cather's fiction, the novel leaves the reader with a sense of community, of wholeness restored. Rejection and mistrust have been offset by reunion and reassurance. That does not mean in this case that Cather condones the evils of the antebellum southern society; she does not. But she does value individual traits and characteristics within it, including some of Sapphira's. The novel leaves us with a picture of forgiveness and compensation in addition to Cather's reconciliation with her own morally equivocal past. The bond between Rachel and her parents and, more important, the bond between Nancy and Rachel represent the author's attempt to join her imagination with memory, to revise a pastoral genre that she inherited as a white southern writer.

Despite the imagined female community at the end of the novel—which prefigures Harriette Arnow's concern in *The Doll-maker*—Cather's last novel perhaps more sharply recalls Mitchell's *Gone with the Wind.* Critics' concern with the nostalgic recreation of antebellum society in *Sapphira*, is, I think, legitimate. By ending the novel from the viewpoint of an "innocent" child narrator, the author herself at a young age, Cather can avoid the responsibility of condemnation. The young child has no understanding of her implication in the system and can rejoice untwinged by guilt at the reunion of Till and Nancy. Yet the plot itself never becomes an apologia for Cather's ancestors' participation in slavery. *Sapphira* actually resembles the slave narrative tradition more than the pastoral as it strips the plantation romance of its pleasant veneer. Escape from the southern garden becomes necessary for the white as well as the black woman, as the following chapter on *The Doll-maker* demonstrates.

4. Harriette Arnow's Exile from the Promised Land: *The Dollmaker*

Her foundation was not God but what God had promised
Moses—land; and she sang on, "Is laid for your faith in His
excellent word: What more can He say than to you He hath
said—" What more, oh Lord, what more could a woman ask?
—The Dollmaker

From the opening pages of Harriette Arnow's *The Dollmaker* (1954),
the protagonist Gertie Nevels pursues the yeoman dream of owning and farming her own land. Her resourcefulness and persis-
tence recall Ellen Glasgow's Dorinda more than Willa Cather's
Sapphira since she cannot hire anyone to do her work for her.
Contrary to Dorinda, Gertie's pastoral dream is never realized in
her Kentucky homeland; only when exiled among strangers in
Detroit can she finally establish the autonomy denied by the traditional society she leaves. Unlike many Appalachian heroines, who
are enervated by subsistence farming,[1] Gertie, who works *with* the
land, according to Dorothy Lee, "as agent and partner" (93), is
empowered by her close relationship to nature. Providing food for
her family with the crops she grows is not as crucial as her closely
identifying with the land itself. It is this relationship to and understanding of nature that later allows her to act for her own and her
family's survival in Detroit.

While Gertie's power clearly derives from nature and her
primitivism is positively contrasted to urban sophistication, she is
nonetheless *not* represented as or associated directly with landscape—as are her predecessors in Appalachian fiction by male

writers. Unlike her aristocratic counterpart, the Appalachian or poor white woman character had been the repository both for male erotic fantasy, which in the Deep South was represented by the black woman (i.e., Nancy in *Sapphira and the Slave Girl*), and male desire for a symbol of virtue (the stereotypical white plantation mistress). This contradictory view of the poor white woman is evident in depictions by William Faulkner and Erskine Caldwell. Faulkner's Eula Varner in *The Hamlet* (1940) is simultaneously a progenitor of the new southern order and a symbol of its corrupted desire. Caldwell's Ellie May in *Tobacco Road* (1932) represents a grotesque version of this paradox: her lasciviousness is both repelling and attracting.

Women writers of Appalachian fiction like Mary Noailles Murfree and Rebecca Harding Davis who represented female characters departing from this stereotype were often labeled "local colorists" and dismissed from serious critical consideration. But Carole Ganim has noted how the close connection between nature and character is treated positively by women authors:

> Embedded within the literature written by women about the Appalachian mountains is this kind of identification of body and mind, of nature and spirit, a paradigm of the female union between the concreteness of the physical world and the psychological, philosophical, moral, and political expression of this earth-based existence. (258)

Her observation points to the origins of a *female* "pastoral impulse," one in which the female character's identity is tied to place. That Gertie's journey begins in her rural homeland is crucial; like Glasgow's and Mitchell's protagonists, she is as much "possessed by" as "possessing of" land.

But as in Cather's southern pastoral, Arnow's rural world is finally a place of victimization, not idealization, of women. Despite the novel's opening celebration of agrarian life, it is a far cry from the traditional nostalgic pastoral or the twentieth-century male

version of the ruined southern garden. Even after the Agrarians of
the 1930s, southern male writers continued to write in the nostaglic
or gothic vein in such novels as Robert Penn Warren's *Meet Me in
the Green Glen* (1971), which not only shows the sexual violation of
a white woman but also confirms both the lack of sympathy and
the generation of hostility between black and white female victims.
In Warren's novel, the heroine's Italian paramour is considered a
"nigger lover" and his dark skin and sexual prowess make him a
symbol for the community of the typical black rapist. This plot is
further complicated by the introduction of a rival—a mulatto
woman. Competing with her for the attention of her Italian lover,
Cassie, the white woman protagonist, kills the woman's husband.

Arnow challenges this representation of hostility between black
and white women with her Appalachian protagonist. Early in *The
Dollmaker*, the author makes a metaphorical link between the black
and poor white women's experiences through Gertie's encounter
with a fellow traveler on the train to Detroit. Gertie talks with a
"brown woman" about the gardens they might be able to grow in
the city and suddenly realizes that she is talking with a black
woman:

> She had never seen a Negro until, in Cincinnati, they had left their
> separate places and mingled with the whites. . . . This woman did
> not look the way she had thought a Negro would—pure black with
> great thick lips and a mashed-down nose. Her skin was brown and
> full of gleams that made Gertie think of the cherry wood. Her eyes
> were large below a high, thin-templed forehead; and when she
> looked at Gertie all her face and the proudful way she held her
> head were somehow queenly . . . (150–51)

By associating the woman's skin with cherry wood, Gertie actually
humanizes rather than naturalizes her. She comprehends difference by reconstructing experience into her own language from
the rural world. Relating the woman to the block of wood also
prefigures Gertie's recognition at the end of the novel that any

face would do to represent Christ (599). Although Elizabeth Schultz stresses the briefness of this conversation and its failure to lead to lasting friendship (75), Gertie's encounter here makes an important class link between women that should not be discounted. Not only does Gertie recognize the black woman's common humanity, she also realizes that they share the same dream for land and a better life for their children. When Gertie pulls out her knife to start whittling, she momentarily frightens her seatmate, an ironic reversal of the typical white fear of black violence. This scene not only establishes an important alliance between oppressed peoples but foreshadows Gertie's experience of community with the women in the alley.

The beginning of the novel also reverses the convention of the passive female. In the first scene Gertie saves her son Amos from choking to death on his own phlegm by cutting a hole in his throat and inserting a whittled stick to create an air passage. The officer and soldier, whom she has stopped by the side of the road in order to demand a ride to the doctor, stand by dumbfounded and helpless. Her primitive tools suffice better than modern technology (the car, the hospital in town) to rescue her child, and her quick action reverses the role of the female bystander in an emergency that calls for male "heroic" action.[2] Significantly, when Amos is finally hospitalized, and Clovis arrives and remarks, "I hope you didn't have to stand an watch that doctor cut that hole" (35), she cannot admit that it is she, not the doctor, who performed the essential operation on their son. Her courageous, unflinching action might contrast unfavorably with her husband's squeamishness.

In fact, despite her motherhood, Gertie is pictured more as "masculine" than "feminine" throughout the novel. The other women of the community depend on her to do heavy lifting while the men are gone to war. As she lifts a sack of feed at the store Gertie replies, "I'll reckon I'll have to be th' man in this settlement" (102). Physically she is large enough to dress in men's overalls and shoes, and "the tanned, weather-beaten skin of her high cheekbones and jutting nose and chin like a brown freckled mask" (17) do not conform to the "natural" feminine beauty of the stereotypical Appalachian heroine, often represented as a fragile flower or blossom.[3] As she sits in church, "[h]er thighs, that could endure the jolting of a mule's back or long hours on the iron seat of the . . . mowing machine, cried to her . . . at their confinement in the encircling bands of knitted or crocheted lace and tucks . . ." (69). Neither female clothing nor the "typical" female activities of sewing and cooking fit Gertie's body or temperament.

While her physical strength and farming abilities allow her to assume her husband's role as head of the household in all but name, Gertie is never granted its concomitant patriarchal authority. Finally, her assumed role in her homeland becomes a trap. She can never assert the power or knowledge she gains as long as society does not recognize or value it.

The author's first novel, *Mountain Path* (1936), presents the paradigm for the Arnow protagonist: although the young schoolteacher, Louisa, leaves the urban world to travel to a rural community, the pattern mirrors Gertie's experience. In the mountain community where Louisa goes to teach school, wives and mothers have little control or influence over the long standing feud among the male moonshiners. Corie Cal, the mountain woman with whom Louisa boards, is depicted as strong and self-sufficient, a nascent Gertie, but she is helpless in the face of male violence. Later in the urban, industrial world of Detroit, Gertie experiences the same helplessness when Clovis becomes involved in union disputes. Gertie *appears* self-sufficient in Kentucky, but like Corie Cal, when conflict develops, her fragile authority is overruled. It seems that Gertie's autonomy in the rural world is too aberrant; Arnow cannot sustain imaginatively the equal roles between her and Clovis and thus changes the scene.

Neither the rural nor the urban world is idealized in *The Doll-maker*.[4] A constant tension between the two makes it impossible to determine which is more viable for Gertie's development. Her ownership of a farm would have cast her even more into the role of an iconoclast, and her self-sufficiency would have been possible only during the war. Lee Edwards claims that, in fact, Gertie's independence is actually "an artifact of war." Afterwards, the traditional patriarchal structure would be reinstalled (225).

But more important, had Gertie never left Kentucky, she would still be subject to the community's insistence on a God of retribution rather than mercy. Gertie's interpretation of Christ contrasts sharply with that of her mother and the rest of the community who follow the "fire and brimstone" preacher, Battle John. Sally Kitch examines Gertie's use of what Lacan terms pre-Oedipal or *imaginaire* elements of language and suggests that this form of language "may contain clues to the repressed female psyches of both character and authors" (67). The patriarchal religion of Gertie's mother and of many in her community is one of the forms of "oppressive discourse" Gertie must confront. Gertie's mother warns her, "You ought to read your Bible. . . . It's all foretold. 'I come not with peace but with a sword . . .'" (64), whereas Gertie sees Christ in nature as a guiding, ever-present spirit.

As the novel progresses, Gertie's inability to counter others' views of the world, whether of the divinity or, later in Detroit, of its societal structure, hinders her autonomy. We witness this silencing from the moment her mother cajoles her into accompanying Clovis to Detroit. Learning of Gertie's purchase of the Tipton land, her mother reproaches her:

> . . . oh, Lord, she's turned her own children against their father.
> She's never taught them th Bible where it says, "Leave all else an
> cleave to thy husband." She's never read to them th words writ by
> Paul,"Wives, be in subjection unto your husbands, as unto th Lord"
> (141).

In such traditional societies, women often show the least amount of sympathy for each other. Gertie's mother wants to force her to conform to the role she had to play as helpmate rather than provider, just as Scarlett O'Hara's mother in *Gone with the Wind* tries to train her to accept a life relegated to the private realm. In both cases, women carry out the patriarchal strictures and mores that the society determines.

But why does Arnow remove her protagonist from her rural homeland just when she is about to acquire the means to secure her autonomy and overcome the demands of a patriarchal society? Unlike Dorinda Oakley in *Barren Ground,* or even Rachel Blake in *Sapphira and the Slave Girl,* Gertie does not have to leave the South in order to break free from her traditional role; she has already. What benefit could the urban, industrialized society possibly offer the female protagonist?

Part of the answer to Arnow's denying Gertie rural independence might lie in the author's experiment with genre. Glenda Hobbs has noted how *Mountain Path* is a take-off on the traditional sentimental mountain story where the educated outsider learns empathy for the crude but heartwarming rural community ("Starting Out in the Thirties" 151), and Kathleen Walsh analyzes *Hunter's Horn,* Arnow's second novel, as a reworking of the quest plot or typical Appalachian hunting tale. *The Dollmaker,* in this sense, can be seen as an experiment in reversing the pastoral plot: instead of the intruder invading "Eden" to deflower the young maiden, as Shelby notes, Arnow takes the mountain people to the urban North to overcome their "innocence" (49).

One consequence of removing the female protagonist from the pastoral world is the change in the representation of the poor, rural woman as sexual victim. Alternately described as masculine and maternal, Gertie is safe from seduction, yet her daughters might still be subject to male betrayal were the Nevels to remain in Kentucky. In fact this is what happens in the earlier *Hunter's Horn* (1949), which is ostensibly about a man's obsession to kill an almost mythic red fox named King Devil but actually gives a clearer picture of the plight of poor women in Appalachia. This novel

foregrounds women's suffering in childbirth, and the plot's resolution is accomplished with the seduction of the hero's daughter,
Suse, who is forced into early marriage rather than realizing her
dream of a high-school education. In the rural world the quest
plot remains male.

The problem with absenting the female protagonist from the
rural world to eliminate her embodiment as a naturalized sex
object is that her sexuality might become denied altogether as it is
in Gertie's case. Gertie seems to be completely unaware of herself
as a sexual being. Her relationship to the land is not mystical or
sensual as is Dorinda's or Scarlett's. No evidence (besides the
existing children) of a sexual relationship between Gertie and
Clovis is ever given. Perhaps representing Gertie's sexuality would
threaten the development of her autonomy as it does for Glasgow's
Ada Fincastle in *Vein of Iron*.

Just as the protagonist has no overt sexuality, so sex is never
broached in the novel itself but hovers at the margins of the plot.
No longer recognized as victims, Gertie's urban women neighbors
suffer in silence. Mrs. Anderson swallows pink medicine in order
to cope with reluctant motherhood; Mrs. Daly pretends pride in
her ever-growing brood of children, and Max saves and plans a
getaway from her "baby killing" husband. Even Clytie, a freshman
in high school, must be wary of the male threat, for as she tells her
mother, she knows how to handle the boys in cars who offer her
rides after school (520). Finally, Maggie Daly, at age seventeen the
most vulnerable to male seduction, decides to enter a convent
rather than marry and fulfill her mother's dream. Her fate is a
sharp contrast to Arnow's earlier portrait of seventeen-year-old
Suse Ballew in *Hunter's Horn*, whose sexual vulnerability is discovered too late—not until she becomes pregnant.

Not in danger of sexual violation herself, Gertie is still victimized by the female role she is forced to assume in Detroit. Unlike
her neighbor Sophronie who works on a factory shift, Gertie must
depend completely on the inconsistent salary that Clovis brings in

and buy on credit, thus losing the earning power and authority she had in Kentucky. Role specialization in the industrial society makes it impossible for her to be both breadwinner and mother. In addition, her "masculine" traits become a hindrance rather than an asset in this new world. Clovis reminds her "that she [is] too big for the factory machinery, set up for little slim women" (253), and her physical size also causes her to move uncomfortably in her own kitchen. She often bumps into drawers and trips over objects. Physically and psychologically, Gertie is ill-suited to the urban world.

Removing the threat of one kind of sexual victimization by "urbanizing" the female pastoral actually only heightens the tension between the sexes. Perhaps contributing more to the Nevelses' tragedy than any other factor (such as Gertie's mother's insistence that her daughter dutifully follow her husband to Detroit) is the miscommunication or lack of communication between Gertie and Clovis. Gertie never tells him about her plan to buy the Tipton place because she believes "he'd want the money for a bigger and better truck" (84). Only after Cassie's death does she discover that he had shared her dream: "Why, if I'd ha knowed you'd has had all that money, I'd said buy a place an wait fer me" (426). On his part, had Clovis written to Gertie before he went to Detroit, the family's move to the city and their spiral downward to poverty could have been avoided.

With the portrayal of their marriage, Arnow remains true to the stereotype of Appalachian character: the reticence she portrays between the two compares to the difficulty of verbal communication between Glasgow's Ada and Ralph in *Vein of Iron*. When asked about the bleak ending of the novel, Arnow mentioned that the difficulty in communication was a main reason for its tragic conclusion: "Gertie's big fault," she replied, "was that she was too secretive. She never told her husband she wanted land or anything else" (Miller 86). Unlike Glasgow, Arnow never imagines a marriage of friendship or partnership like that between Dorinda and

Nathan in *Barren Ground*. In the industrialized urban world, both Ada and Ralph and Gertie and Clovis lose the ability to share tasks and burdens. Even the makeshift doll factory they set up is more directed by Clovis than a joint project. Gertie participates, but unwillingly. The failure of communication between Gertie and Clovis underlies the denial of the female pastoral dream—a revisioned rural community of cooperative work and responsibility.

Moreover, the differing viewpoints of men and women are writ large in the alley world. Detroit highlights not only a contrast of urban versus rural values but also male versus female, for even in rural Kentucky, as Arnow depicts in her two earlier novels, men perpetuate bloody feuds and jealous competition in hunting. The snowball fights in the Nevelses' project are initiated by boys who are already socialized into the violence of their fathers.

But while their husbands are competing for economic survival in factory jobs, the women learn to care for each other's children and to share emotional burdens. When Sophronie comes home drunk and tries to dye her daughter's hair with food coloring, the women in the housing project act as a team, caring for the incoherent Sophronie, looking after her children, and washing the child's hair with bleach. True, the vitriolic Mrs. Daly exhibits almost as much prejudice as her bigoted husband, but she also expresses genuine empathy for her Japanese neighbor when she learns about the bombing of Nagasaki:

> When u first bomb fell, I wasn't certain right away—I got tu thinking—that is . . . I ain't never seen mu mudder's country, onie what she'd tell to me, but . . . yu still gotta say, people is people. Why them Japs lives something like this . . . all crowded up tugedder inu towns; little cardboard houses kinda like what we've got; and maybe lotsa—you know—kids. (496)

Gradually the women of the project draw together, in contrast to the men who succumb to quarreling and violence in order to preserve their jobs. Clovis's appropriation of Gertie's carving knife to take revenge on his unknown assailant is symbolic of the destructive use of the same tool Gertie once used to save her son Amos's life in Kentucky. The women work against the fragmentation of industrial society by creating bonds across racial and cultural barriers. They watch each other's children and offer condolences and food during illness and unemployment.

These female characters are not alienated urbanites or fallen aristocrats mourning a past feudalism but are participants in a working-class community. Arnow's pastoral vision, like that of Cather's and Glasgow's, becomes a form of protest rather than a nostalgic defense of a past way of life. Arnow herself explained in an interview:

> . . . when [Gertie] reached the alley in Detroit, she found all manner of people. She herself might be called 'hillbilly' and the children might fight, but they all fought—but she became part of the conglomeration of people and in a sense she was more at home . . . she knew more kindness from her neighbors when she was in trouble. Even from the beginning when the neighbor man the children awakened offered kindling, and Mrs. Murphy's daughter brought an old toy bed or something and grease to start the fire. No one would have thought of giving Gertie kindling at home, or of helping her in any way. . . . She ceased to be the peculiar person that didn't fit into the community— that's the way I saw it—but was a part of all these strange people. (Miller 86–87)

The Dollmaker forms this vision of cooperative community, as does Arnow's more recent novel *The Weedkiller's Daughter* (1970), by showing the effects of the transference of rural, communal values to a capitalistic, industrial society.[5] In the earlier novel, the rise of consumerism and credit buying, aptly illustrated by the Neveleses' purchase of the "Icy Heart," an almost anthropomorphic refrigerator monster, coupled with the exploitation of unskilled laborers in post–World War II society, destroys self-sufficiency and threatens these values. In *The Weedkiller's Daughter*, the untrammeled growth of suburbs and the resultant ecological damage create xenophobia and classism by separating people from their rural heritage.

The Dollmaker demonstrates that, despite the cooperation among the women in the housing project, communal values are ultimately ineffective in a capitalistic world which favors bitter rivalry over compassion. The women's community formed at Merry Hill is a temporary reaction to crisis and, like most women's groups, not sanctioned or institutionalized like male organizations. Nina Auerbach explains that such communities provide a "corporate and contradictory vision of a unit that is simultaneously defective and transcendent" (5).[6] In other words, the women in the alley will support one another as long as they can circumvent their husband's authority, but their ultimate loyalty still rests with the official unit of patriarchal control: the nuclear family. Lasting friendship across class and race boundaries seems impossible in Arnow's urban community.

Yet another reason for removing Gertie from her Kentucky homeland is to establish *The Dollmaker* in the Künstlerroman tradition in which the artist must leave her or his homeland in order to find identity. Arnow demonstrates, however, as do other women writers from Kate Chopin to Willa Cather, what a high price female protagonists must pay in order to realize their artistic identity.[7] In this sense, Gertie must choose between her family and her art. Her act of "selling out" and returning the money she had once saved to buy the Tipton place not only indicates the sacrifices she must make as a mother but seems to indicate a kind of self-betrayal.

At first Gertie resists the violation of her art—she wants to use several patterns for her dolls instead of mass-producing one—yet mass production becomes the only means of ensuring her family's survival. But even as Gertie's independence and creativity are stripped away, the anguish she experiences allows her to develop her art. After Reuben leaves and Cassie is killed, she works through her grief by carving on the block of wood: she tries to determine if it is Christ or Judas who is latent in the emerging figure, and her art is an attempt to answer this question. As she carves, "gradually, her own torture [becomes] instead the agony of the bowed head in the block of wood" (444). Her muse comes from pain rather than joy. Although her relationship with nature enables her to establish her craft, it is separation from the pastoral world that enables her art to surface.

The difficulty women experience in developing a creative self either in a rural or an urban environment is underlined in Gertie's relationship with her daughter Cassie and Cassie's imaginary friend, Callie Lou. In Kentucky, Cassie's behavior is not seen as aberrant. The privacy of the woods and rural landscape allow her self-expression. In Detroit, however, she must conform to the other children's play, and Gertie's destruction of Callie Lou is essentially a destruction of her own art as well. While mourning Cassie, Gertie often sees Callie Lou lurking in the shadows, but she only appears after Gertie takes the pink medicine. In the "real" world of Detroit, a fragile creature of the imagination cannot survive—Callie Lou is the unrealized female artist, Gertie herself.[8]

Much earlier in the novel, when Cassie is playing in the Nevelses' Kentucky house with the block of wood, mother and daughter disagree over the gender of the figure. Cassie claims that it is female—for her it is Callie Lou—while Gertie insists: "He's been a waiten there in th wood you might say before I was born. . . . [O]ne a these days, jist you wait an see, we'll find th time an a face fer him an bring him out a that block" (48). Searching for either a figure of self-sacrifice, Christ, or a betrayer, Judas, Gertie misses the third possibility for a human face—her own. At the end of the novel, when she destroys the block of wood and tells the scrap-wood man that any face "would ha done" to express the anguished figure she has carved, it is hard *not* to see her act as self-sacrificial, for by it she destroys her masterpiece in favor of the jumping jack dolls. Laurence Goldstein observes that her carving "disintegrates into a mimicry of the assembly-line technics that are the signature

of Detroit industry" (279). By quartering the block of wood, it
seems, Gertie finally "adjusts" to urban life.

But why must she pay such a high price for survival? Why does
Arnow allow Gertie only to glimpse and then destroy the product
of her creativity? Why can she not derive a muse from nature? One
answer might lie not so much in the self-sacrifice of Christ as in the
promise God gives to Moses. Gertie, like Moses, and the woman
artist, is an exile in a foreign land. She pays for the "sin" of creativity with her banishment. The reader might suspect all along that
she will never realize her dream of having "a little piece of heaven
right here on earth" (77). The Tipton land, like Israel, is always
just beyond her reach. It is even described more as vision than
reality; walking over the property, Gertie feels as if the grass and
flowers "were set in some land that was forever spring" (56). The
"archetype" of Gertie's journey is exile rather than damnation:
Detroit, as Francis Malpezzi observes, is Babylon, not hell (86).
One of her progeny, Reuben, does reach the promised land when
he runs away back to Kentucky, yet Gertie herself can neither
realize her potential artistry nor pass it on to her daughters.

The vision of the pastoral world remains as an alluring but
impossible dream and, ironically, Arnow presents here the strongest argument for sustaining the female character's identification
with nature. Were Gertie to return to Kentucky after her experience in Detroit, she might be able to assert her newfound autonomy to buy and farm her own land.

In *The Weedkiller's Daughter*, Gertie Nevels reappears as a minor
character, "The Primitive," a recluse who lives on a farm in a
Michigan suburb. She finally achieves her dream of owning land.
When the novel begins, however, her land is already threatened by
encroaching urbanization. Clues in *The Dollmaker* itself also rein-
force the ultimate impossibility of the pastoral dream for Arnow's
Appalachian woman. After the harsh Detroit winter, Gertie plants
a little garden in the alley and her son Enoch tries to protect it
from the ravages of the other children and dogs by building a

fence. The cornflowers are fragile, though, and soon despoiled by the violent Daly boys (466). Symbolically, this little garden is all that is left of Gertie's vision of her past. She must learn to cultivate plants like the desert-hardy cactus that the evicted woman gives to her near the end of the novel.

Despite the failure of Gertie's dream for herself and her family, some critics view the ending of the novel as positive. Dorothy Lee compares Gertie to Christ and values her self-sacrifice for others, while Lee Edwards sees her art as a "crutch" that she must abandon in order to realize her heroism. Her carvings, Edwards asserts, "signify not Gertie's engagement with her new community . . . but rather her inability to deal directly with the terms of the life that she is living" (229). Gertie's recognition of communal values *is* important—the true significance of her journey to the urban world is an indication of a break with her past and a rejection of the role into which her mother would have cast her. Fielding Burke's 1932 novel, *Call Home the Heart*, indicates what happens to the Appalachian woman protagonist who returns home to her farm—she is again subject to the narrow judgment of a rural society that enforces sexual hierarchy.

But, though Gertie's "adjustment" in the end may be a disillusionment, it is not a defeat. Nor is her final gesture one of complete self-sacrifice. There is another way of interpreting the last scene. As much as Gertie's artistry is stifled by the necessity of providing for her family, the difficulty of combining art and motherhood is not, as Glenda Hobbs believes, the main "problem" of the novel ("Portrait" 854–55). Gertie's self-development is furthered rather than hindered by her decision to destroy the block of wood. She has asserted her autonomy and her ability to provide for the welfare of others when her husband cannot. Her work, while not "art," will allow the Nevelses to survive. In fact, by destroying the "artifact," Gertie demonstrates her true understanding of the nature of artistic creation. As in Alice Walker's story "Everyday Use," it is the process of creation, not the end product, that counts most. The art object itself is transitory and can be functional as well as beautiful. It is the knowledge to create art—to make more quilts or carve more figures in wood—that is essential. Forced to forgo an artistic identity, Gertie nonetheless maintains her ability to create art *and* act independently.

Finally, *The Dollmaker* itself, like Arnow's earlier novels, attempts to redefine the conventions of Appalachian fiction. Arnow struggles as much to establish her artistic independence from the prevailing "pastoral impulse" as to reconcile the process of artistic creation with its products.

Early in her career Arnow was persuaded by her publisher to make her first novel, *Mountain Path*, more conventional by incorporating more "drama" in the form of a feud. After she bowed to the wishes of her editor at Covici-Friede, Harold Strauss, not only the author but reviewers were dissatisfied with this element of the plot. It confirmed the stereotypical view of Appalachian communities as violent and primitive. In her next novel, *Between the Flowers*, Arnow tried to rectify this view by depicting more of an individual relationship and its internal conflicts rather than concentrating on dramatic action. Strauss objected to the manuscript as "lacking story value." [9] But Arnow did not alter the plot of her second novel; consequently, it never was published. Perhaps it was not so much its lack of action that distressed Strauss and the publishing houses to which he sent the manuscript, but Arnow's attempt to revise the pastoral plot.

In *Between the Flowers* it is the woman who is restless and dissatisfied with mountain life. Unlike Gertie, young Delph finds no satisfaction in working on the land. At this point in her writing, Arnow had not yet discovered how to create an autonomous female protagonist. Delph resists her destiny as housekeeper/mother, but because she is still pictured as the typical, "naturalized" Appalachian woman—her eyes are described as "a deeper blue than most, snow water clear and forever changing, like deep lakes or rivers . . ." (20)—she lacks the physical strength and will to challenge her traditional role. Until Arnow could connect her female protagonist to the land, not as a representation of nature but as its owner and tamer, she could neither imagine a triumphant outcome of the plot nor avoid complying with her publisher's wishes for revision. Significantly, Delph dies at a young age, her dream of leaving the mountains denied.

Arnow's frustration with her art is reflected in a short story she wrote during the same period. "Fra Lippi and Me" concerns a waitress who overhears a conversation between a young artist and a woman who wants to be his patron. The young man essentially "sells out" by silently assenting to her manipulation of his career, and his artistic integrity is destroyed.[10] Identifying with the young artist, the waitress realizes that she too is about to "sell out" by accepting the easy money of an admirer. Arnow may have seen herself as well in this role: forced to please her "patron" Strauss and unable to express her true artistic voice.

The Dollmaker is the novel in which Arnow finally asserts her independence from her label as "Appalachian" author. By reversing the pastoral plot and tracing Gertie's anguished struggle to realize her selfhood and artistry, the author overcomes two hurdles: she moves beyond the stamp of provinciality given to her fiction, and she creates a viable female protagonist who may "sell out" her artistic masterpiece when she quarters the block of cherry wood but who also severs the tie to her fictional predecessors. Poor white women need no longer be victims (like Suse Ballew in *Hunter's Horn*) or martyrs of endurance and fortitude (like Glasgow's Dorinda Oakley in *Barren Ground*) but can actively pursue their own destinies. Unfortunately, in Arnow's fiction at least, they must leave the southern garden behind in order to do so. The next chapter examines Alice Walker's later *return* to the southern garden to realize the pastoral dream denied to Gertie.

5. Alice Walker's Re-Visioned Rural Community: *The Color Purple*

No one could wish for a more advantageous heritage than
that bequeathed to the black writer in the South: a compassion for the earth, a trust in humanity beyond our knowledge
of evil, and an abiding love of justice. We inherit a great
responsibility as well, for we must give voice to centuries
not only of silent bitterness and hate but also of neighborly
kindness and sustaining love.

> —Alice Walker, "The Black Writer
> and the Southern Experience"

Well, us talk and talk bout God, but I'm still adrift. Trying
to chase that old white man out of my head. I been so busy
thinking bout him I never truly notice nothing God make.
Not a blade of corn . . . not the color purple. . . . Not the
little wildflowers. Nothing. Now that my eyes opening, I feels
like a fool. Next to any little scrub of a bush in my yard,
Mr———'s evil sort of shrink. But not altogether. Still, it is
like Shug say, You have to get man off your eyeball, before
you can see anything a'tall. . . .

> —Celia, *The Color Purple*

Alice Walker's pastoral, *The Color Purple* (1982), moves in an opposite trajectory from Harriette Arnow's earlier urbanized pastoral.
While Arnow suggests escape from the southern garden as solution to prescriptive community codes and female victimization,
Walker, like her predecessors Zora Neale Hurston and Ellen Glasgow, imagines this same garden as liberating and regenerative.
Because the black woman writer had a double burden of oppression to overcome—sexism and racism—it may have taken longer

for her to return to her homeland in order to recreate the pastoral world. In addition, a prevailing literary model in African-American fiction is based upon the slave narrative rather than the plantation romance so that escape from the rural homeland, the South, became a necessary component in character growth.[1] Ralph Ellison's *Invisible Man* (1952) epitomizes this genre.[2]

Another reason the black pastoral may have evolved later is that, unlike white novelists in the first half of the twentieth century, most black writers wanted to distance themselves from their past in order to assimilate into mainstream American life. Contemporary novelist Toni Morrison admitted in an interview that she deliberately sets her novels in her native Ohio because it "offers an escape from stereotyped black settings. It is neither plantation nor ghetto" (Claudia Tate 119). Novels by Nella Larsen and Jessie Fauset in the 1920s concentrate on the urban, black middle class rather than traditional folk culture in order to circumvent these stereotypes. Larsen's *Passing* (1929) and Fauset's *Plum Bun* (1928) and *The Chinaberry Tree* (1931) follow this pattern. At the end of Larsen's *Quicksand* (1928), heroine Helga Crane actually moves to the rural South to marry—and consequently encounters a life of drudgery. This conclusion parallels novels about Appalachian women heroes in the same period like Edith Summers Kelley's *Weeds* (1923) and, in its journey north and back, Fielding Burke's *Call Home the Heart* (1932). None of these authors could imagine a positive rural experience for women.

For some novelists of this period, though, notably Jean Toomer and Zora Hurston, reintegration into the rural community became an important, if often unsatisfactory, motif. Some forty years later, Alice Walker, who acknowledges Hurston as literary foremother, celebrated the possibility of female autonomy and bonding among black rural women in *The Color Purple*. Yet Walker's novel begins where Hurston's *Their Eyes Were Watching God* ends. In the earlier novel, a tentative female community is visualized only between Jane and Pheoby as Janie recounts her life with Tea Cake to her friend. Much of the novel still centers on the romantic plot. Walker's novel presents the problems of a sexist society more graphically and portrays actual change in the black rural community. The author returns to the "folk" not only to reclaim her heritage, as Hurston does, but to envision a better society for both women and men. By recasting the populist myth of the independent farmer, she can imagine a more communal rural world.

Bettye J. Parker-Smith observes that, for Walker, "the South provides a spiritual balance and an ideological base from which to construct her characters" (478). In fact, all the author's novels are set in the South, although it is not until *The Color Purple* that she is able to imagine a pastoral world that can be transformed from oppressive to triumphant.[3] *The Third Life of Grange Copeland* (1970), Walker's first novel, like Glasgow's and Cather's early fiction, concerns the spiritual growth of a male protagonist; the women are still too trapped by the oppressive system to realize their own identities. *Meridian* (1976) comes closer to female pastoral by centering on a woman protagonist but it too offers no way out, or rather *up*, for the rural woman. *Grange Copeland* ends by allowing the black male to achieve growth and self-acceptance while the black woman still suffers, and *Meridian* inhibits true friendship between the two women protagonists, Meridian and Lynne, because of the racial barrier.

Struggling with two issues—how to overcome sexism and racism—Walker finally decided to treat them sequentially rather than simultaneously. In *The Color Purple*, consequently, she focuses on the black community and deals with interracial relationships only through Sofia's role as "mammy" to her white employer. The novel opens with Celie's rape by her mother's husband, who she believes is her biological father. Until the arrival of Shug, male oppression dominates the plot. Albert replaces Celie's father as her "slave driver," forcing her to work in the fields, care for his children, and satisfy his lust. Even Sofia, much stronger physically than her husband Harpo, realizes she must leave in order to avoid a constant battle for control; she tells Celie, "He don't want a wife, he want a dog" (68).

Black male power in this novel clearly derives from the same source as white supremacy—the desire for ownership and control over others' lives. Calvin Hernton notes that "the world of sexism is a copy of the world of racism" (10) and compares the patriarchal oppression of the women characters with the Jim Crow laws of the South they inhabit. Albert "owns" Celie in the sense that he can control all but her thoughts. Like the black tenant farmer, she has no choice but to work for her "master." Worse than his physical abuse of her is his ability to isolate her from other women. Not only is she separated from her sister, but Celie becomes so indoctrinated into this system of male oppression that she helps perpetuate it for Harpo's new bride:

> I like Sofia, but she don't act like me at all. If she talking when Harpo and Mr. —— come in the room she keep right on. . . . I think bout this when Harpo ast me what he ought to do to her to make her mind. I don't mention how happy he is now. . . . I think bout how every time I jump when Mr. —— call me, she look surprise. And like she pity me. Beat her. I say. (38)

This response parallels Till's attitude in Cather's *Sapphira and the Slave Girl;* both women accept oppression as "normal" to the extent that any breach of this code becomes suspect or taboo. Just as Till would betray her own daughter to avoid disobeying her mistress, so Celie tells Harpo to beat Sofia in order to punish her for her lack of respect for her would-be oppressor husband. Finally, Albert even deprives Celie of her letters from Nettie. Like Brownfield in *Grange Copeland* who forces his wife to forget her educated language, he maintains control through completely ostracizing Celie from the outside world. He keeps her sister Nettie's letters from her for years, and Celie is forced to write letters to God in secret without hope of a response. The epistolary format of the novel, though, Lindsey Tucker explains, provides a key to

Celie's eventual growth to selfhood (82). As she recovers/discovers her "voice" through writing, she learns to assert her own identity. This occurs much later, however, only after the arrival of Albert's lover Shug.

As a result of her isolation, Celie never questions Albert's commands, even as he prepares for a tryst with Shug: "I move round darning and ironing, finding hanskers. Anything happening? I ast. What you mean? he say, like he mad. Just trying git some of the hick farmer off myself. Any other woman be glad. I'm is glad, I say. . . . You looks nice, I say. Any woman be proud. . . ." (25). The point is that Celie doesn't see herself as a *woman*. She has been reduced to an object. She writes, "I make myself wood," and says to herself, "Celie, you a tree" (23), in order to deny both her anger and her pain. When Nettie, Albert's sister Kate, and Sofia successively urge her to fight back, she responds the same each time: "What good it do? I don't fight, I stay where I'm told. But I'm alive" (22). Her marriage is a form of bondage akin to slavery, and survival becomes the only option.[4]

When Shug arrives, Celie becomes her "slave" as well, nursing her back to health in order to win approval from her new "mistress." Far from becoming another oppressor Shug becomes Celie's spiritual enabler, just as Celie helps her to get back on her feet physically. She helps Celie recognize her sexual identity and, once made aware of Albert's abuse, she tells her: "I won't leave . . . until I know Albert won't even think about beating you" (79). Slowly, she begins to show Celie the process by which she can reach selfhood and establish self-worth. First, she dedicates a song to Celie at Harpo's new juke joint. "First time somebody made something and name it after me," Celie writes to God (77). According to Melvin Dixon, Shug's singing of the blues in the novel is a redemptive act (107). Even more important is her teaching Celie how to celebrate God in nature:

> I believe God is everything, say Shug. . . . My first step from the old white man was trees. Then air. Then birds. Then other people. But

one day when I was sitting quiet and feeling like a motherless
child, which I was, it come to me: that feeling of being part of
everything, not separate at all. And I knew that if I cut a tree, my
arm would bleed. And I laughed and I cried and I run all around
the house . . . . It sort of like you know what, she say, grinning and
rubbing high up on my thigh. (203)

Unlike Celie, Shug recognizes and values a tree as a living being.
Walker calls this kind of faith *animism*—"a belief that makes it pos–
sible to view all creation as living, as being inhabited by spirit"
(qtd. in Shelton 391). It enables Shug, and finally Celie, to appre–
ciate and respect her own worth as well as others.

This love of nature is symbolized in the novel by the color
purple. As Shug admonishes Celie: "I think it pisses God off if you
walk by the color purple in a field somewhere and don't notice it"
(203). Melvin Dixon explains that Walker uses purple to signal
transformation in the novel, not only from low self-esteem to self-
possession but from the wilderness of despair to "an abiding respect for cultivated landscapes: gardens" (105).[5] The color purple
may also be a deliberate means of "signifying" from Hurston's
earlier pastoral *Their Eyes Were Watching God.*[6] Hurston uses Janie's
experience with the blossoms of a pear tree and the trope of the
horizon to evoke her protagonist's growing self-awareness. Walker,
likewise, literally dresses Celie in purple to emphasize her self-
empowerment through nature.

Women characters' connection to the land in the female pastoral, or, in this instance, nature as a whole, signals their ability to
develop autonomy. Like her fictional predecessors, Glasgow's
Dorinda and Hurston's Janie, Shug celebrates nature but is not a
"naturalized" heroine. She can derive sensuality and sexuality from
her connection to it. Proof of this enabling, creative link with
nature is her status as a blues singer and her ability to foster
others' talent. Shug encourages Celie to make her folkspants, and
she also launches Mary Agnes's singing at the juke joint.

But even Shug remains susceptible to society's definition of woman as sexual object. Arriving at Albert's for Christmas, she brings a surprise—a new husband—and tells Celie, "Us two married ladies now" (113). Her marriage to Grady is a search for respectability, an attempt to play the role of a conventional woman. More serious is her treatment of Annie Julia, Albert's first wife, which she realizes in retrospect was wrong: "She never had a chance. I was so mean, and so wild, Lord. I used to go round saying, I don't care who he married to, I'm gonna fuck him" (127). Annie Julia's plight is the same as Margaret's in *Grange Copeland*: both are victimized by motherhood for they must remain at home while their husbands roam the town, and both, in feeble acts of rebellion, take lovers who eventually cause their death. Celie, however, escapes this fate, not only because Shug has learned from her former disregard of other women, but also because she is actually not a mother—her biological children are sent to Africa, allowing her to develop her own identity in their absence. Like Hurston's Janie and Glasgow's Dorinda, Celie is spared the responsibility of *bearing* children although both she and Dorinda do become stepmothers.

   The Color Purple further revises the traditional pastoral plot of female victimization by challenging the myth of female beauty. From the moment Celie's stepfather literally sells her to Albert as "used goods," she believes, as men tell her, that she is ugly. Shug's first comment to her is: "You sure *is* ugly" (48), an opinion which she reverses once she learns to love Celie but which also indicates how ingrained the white male standards of beauty are. The lighter the skin, the straighter the hair, the more a woman resembled the southern-belle stereotype and the more she was prized.

   Walker comments on this tendency to elevate the mulatto heroine over her darker sister in her essay, "If the Present Looks Like the Past, What Does the Future Look Like?" Consistently in her own fiction, however, she questions this depiction of female beauty although she avoids deriding the light skinned woman for her status: "That black men choose light and white women is not the women's fault, any more than it was their fault they were chosen as concubines to rich plantation owners during slavery" (*Our Mothers' Gardens* 307). According to Walker, placing value judgments upon one's skin tone not only is colorism, and thus divisive, but further allows men, black and white, to create tension and competition between women.

Hazel Carby has analyzed how the representation of the black woman character developed in relation to the patriarchal ideology of white female sexuality. She explains that "two very different but interdependent codes of sexuality operated in the antebellum South producing opposing definitions of motherhood and womanhood for white and black women which coalesce in the figures of the slave and the mistress." Black women writers, Carby maintains, have "addressed, used, transformed and on occasion subverted the dominant ideological codes" (*Reconstructing Womanhood* 20–21). Although she discusses an earlier period in African-American literature, Carby's point is still relevant to Walker. Changing the representation of one stereotype without the other cannot revolutionize the system. Black women characters, in particular, can evolve from their representation as sexually promiscuous and debased only if their white counterparts are no longer viewed as the repository of "true womanhood," i.e., sexual purity.

Early twentieth-century black women writers dealt with this problem of sexual depravity by imitating patterns in nineteenth-century domestic fiction by white women which emphasized chastity and domesticity. The "tragic mulatto" motif created in reconstruction fiction was used by Harlem Renaissance writers to show how a virtuous black woman might be led astray. To depict a black female protagonist with sexual desire was even more problematic than showing a white woman character in the same manner. Nella Larsen's protagonists show the difficulty of disassociating the black heroine from this sexual stereotype. In *Quicksand*, Helga Crane struggles between her desire to fulfill her sexual passion and the necessity of appearing "ladylike": she is caught in a quagmire of conflicting ideologies. On the one hand, in order to avoid the label of being a "loose" woman, she can associate with aspiring middle-class blacks like Dr. Anderson who repress sexual passion and ape white culture. On the other hand, if she chooses to seek sexual fulfillment—as she does in her ecstatic religious conversion and sudden acceptance of marriage to the preacher Mr. Pleasant Green—she is doomed to the life of continual childbearing and domestic drudgery. Larsen, like other black women writers of her period, was afraid to present Helga's unbridled sexual passion lest she unwittingly conform to the stereotype of the "primitive exotic."[7]

In *The Color Purple* the "tragic mulatto" theme is recast in the encounter between Sofia and Mary Agnes. A "yellow" woman, Mary Agnes is portrayed as weak and mousy compared to the confident, powerful Sofia who easily defeats her husband's mistress in a battle at the juke joint. But the point that Walker makes in this confrontation is not that the dark woman *can* win, but that finally color doesn't matter. Later in the novel the two become friends. Mary Agnes cares for Sofia's children while she is in jail. Once they both defy the male strategy that would pit them as enemies, beauty and possession of the "prize" man no longer matter.

With Celie and Shug's relationship, Walker further revises the myth of female beauty. When they first meet, Shug still conforms to the colorist view. Celie notices: "Under all that powder her face black as Harpo. She got a long pointed nose and big fleshy mouth. Lips look black plum. Eyes big, glossy. . . ." (48). Shug is *not*—as the film portrays her—a light-skinned woman. She is beautiful because she exudes sexuality; as Celie observes: "All the men got their eyes glued to Shug's bosom. I got my eyes glued there too. I feel my nipples harden under my dress. . . . I say to her in my mind, Girl, you looks like a real good time. . ." (85). By showing Celie how to be aware of her own sexuality, Shug enables her to believe in her inherent beauty and value. Not only does Celie discover that some-

one else—Shug—can love her emotionally and physically but that
she need not accept the false equation of physical beauty with
admiration and love.

Shug also teaches Celie a new language to express her revised
view of female sexuality. According to Molly Hite:

> (Shug) begins by replacing conventional terminology for the
> female genitals, shifting the emphasis from a hole that requires
> plugging to a button that gets hot and finally melts. . . . [Her]
> redefinition of the word "virgin" is equally threatening to
> patriarchal control over women's bodies, in that it places priority
> not on penetration . . . but on enjoyment, making the woman's
> own response the index of her "experience." (128)

As well as signaling Celie's assertion of her identity, the epistolary
form of the narrative allows the development and expression of
this "women's language." Whereas Janie Crawford's story is undercut by silence at such crucial points as when Tea Cake beats her,
Celie's letters subvert patriarchal discourse. Not only does she
begin renaming and redefining experience, she gains the authority to tell her own tale unmediated by the author or the conventional romantic plot.

The same hierarchy of racial and sexual oppression is present
in the African sections of the novel. While Nettie witnesses the
terrible effects of a patriarchal society on Tashi, Adam's Olinka
lover, who submits to the tribal ceremony of female initiation by
having her face cut, she also sees the destruction of the Olinka
village when the white imperialists arrive to cut a road through it.
The interests of a patriarchal English rubber manufacturer over-
ride all others.

Just as we are given a female version of experience through
Celie's use of women's language, so we witness the African view of
the arrival of the white imperialists who show no respect for the
land. To the Africans, "Adam" is not the first human created to
inhabit the Garden of Eden, but the first *white* man. Black is the

normal or natural color, and white is an aberration for the Olinka. As Celie retells the story:

> They say everybody before Adam was black. Then one day some woman they just right away kill, come out with this colorless baby. They thought at first it was something she ate. But then another one had one also the women start to have twins. So the people start to put the white babies and twins to death. So really Adam wasn't even the first white man. He was just the first one the people didn't kill. (280)

Walker undermines the idea of white supremacy through this reversal of the Edenic myth. Her most recent novel, *The Temple of My Familiar* (1989), continues to revise this white, western version of human origins. In doing so, Walker calls into question the patriarchal assumptions of the African colonizers.

In another sense, however, the Olinka village is a copy of Celie's world in America. Discussing *The Color Purple* with Gloria Steinem, Walker said, "We're going to have to debunk the myth that Africa is a heaven for black people—especially black women. We've been the mule of the world there and the mule of the world here" (273). And Nettie comments in a letter to her sister: "I think Africans are very much like white people back home, in that they think they are the center of the universe and that everything that is done is done for them . . ." (174), which means that they assume that everyone has an interest in the status quo—a dangerous view according to Walker. As a result, the Olinka never question their own customs, and mutual misunderstanding between the sexes continues. Sexual oppression is as much the African way of life as it is American. Nettie writes: "But many of the women rarely spend time with their husbands. Some of them were promised to old or middle-aged men at birth. Their lives always center around work and their children and other women . . ." (172). Here, the potential danger of an exclusive women's community is also revealed.

But, although Nettie celebrates women's friendships, she is

quick to observe that the men's childishness and oppressiveness is often fostered by the way their wives treat them—they indulge their husbands instead of communicating with them. This same danger exists for the women in Celie's community. Unless they somehow reach reconciliation with the men, the cycle of abuse and misunderstanding can never be stopped.

At the end of the novel, Walker does offer the possibility of healing and communication between men and women with the reconciliation between Celie and Albert. The two sit out on the porch together sewing and talking. Celie declines his offer of marriage—the first time he asks her instead of "buying" her from her stepfather—but accepts his companionship. Albert designs a shirt pattern to go with Celie's folkspants. Like Dorinda and Nathan, the two share a mutual interest. Walker replays Glasgow's scene with Dorinda and Nathan out on the porch when Celie writes to Nettie: "Here us is, I thought, two old fools left over from love, keeping each other company under the stars" (278). She uses Cather's "portrait" technique to depict still-life moments that compensate for the failure of words and actions. Reconciliation between the men and women of the community is told rather than enacted. When Nettie, Samuel, and Celie's grown children finally return from Africa, Albert, Shug, and Celie stand together on the porch to greet the voyagers, symbolizing harmony and forgiveness.

Yet even though the black women of the novel bond together to oppose their shared oppression by black men, no possibility for interracial friendship among women exists. Black and white women live in worlds too far apart in the Jim Crow South. Sofia's internment, first in prison, then as "mammy" to a white family, reveals the degree to which whites hold racist views that prevent understanding among women. Sofia's employers have no conception of what her life is like outside and when her day off is cut short by Miz Millie's inability to drive her car, not a word of apology is spoken.

This scene shows how the racism in the novel goes even deeper than the sexism. When Sofia offers her sister's husband as chauffeur to accompany Miz Millie back to town, the white woman backs off in fear, "Oh, she say, I couldn't ride in a pick-up with a strange colored man" (110), and she won't even consent to have another woman go along. Earlier, battling the oppression of white supremacy finally unites black men and women. When Sofia is first sent to prison, the black community gathers together to consider how to get her out. It is one of the only moments of agreement between the sexes in the novel, but it is significant because it reveals the underlying elements of all oppression—physical and sexual control. Mary Agnes goes to the jail to confront her white uncle with the evidence of his miscegenation—herself. Unlike her ability to overcome Harpo's dominance (after this incident she makes him call her by her real name instead of "Squeak" and begins to pursue her singing in earnest), she is not able to fight racial oppression successfully. The warden rapes her in order to demonstrate his authority: no black can threaten him with blackmail.

Walker's pastoral thus seems to envision little hope for inter–racial understanding. She "solves" the problem of sexual oppression with the introduction of Shug, a character who transforms relationships and myths of sexual identity to enable the black community to live in equality. Shug never participates in the larger, white world, however. Only Sofia does, and her experience is not encouraging. Even after she leaves the employment of Miz Millie, the white children of the family still view her as "mammy," especially Eleanor Jane who calls her whenever a crisis occurs. At one point Eleanor Jane asks Sofia point blank to affirm that she *just* loves her "sweet, smart cute, *innocent* little baby boy," and Sofia is finally honest: "No ma'am, say Sofia. I do not love Reynolds Stanley Earl. Now. That's what you been trying to find out ever since he was born . . ." (271). When Eleanor Jane responds that she won't "let him be mean to colored," Sofia is even more direct: "You and whose army? The first word he likely to speak won't be nothing he learn from you. . . . I'm telling you *I* won't be able to love your own son. You can love him just as much as you want to. But be ready to suffer the consequences. That's how the colored live" (273).

After this encounter, Eleanor Jane finally begins to understand how she participates in a racist system. Near the end of the novel she takes care of Sofia's child Henrietta while Sofia works in Celie's store, reversing the nurturing that was always done for her. Celie asks how this transformation occurred:

> Oh, say Sofia. It finally dawn on her to ast her mama why I come to work for them. I don't expect it to last, though, say Harpo. You know how they is. Do her peoples know? I ast. They know, say Sofia. They carrying on just like you know they would. Whoever heard of a white woman working for niggers, they rave. She tell them, Whoever heard of somebody like Sofia working for trash. (288)

Although Eleanor Jane and Sofia will never be friends, the learning process has clearly begun. Furthermore, from this exchange it seems that trust will be built first among women—Harpo still doubts Eleanor Jane's "conversion."

By depicting the reintegration of a black community that can exist independently of the white racist society, Walker makes an affirmative statement about black southern life in *The Color Purple*. She moves from depicting the "silent bitterness and hate" that dominate her earlier novels to portraying the "neighborly kindness and sustaining love" she sees as unique to the black southern experience (*Our Mothers' Gardens* 21). The women characters in the novel overcome sexual oppression through Shug's example. Celie learns how to view herself *not* as victim, but as an independent, creative woman. Typical of the female pastoral, she draws her sexual identity and creativity *from* nature rather than becoming identified with it. Creativity brings liberation—she can also support herself financially by selling her folkspants. Her work/art is a kind of sexual energy in itself, like Dorinda's and Gertie's passion for the land.

Hovering at the edges of the black female pastoral, however, remains the threat of the white world. Walker, with Zora Neale Hurston's celebration of female sexuality as a model, was not as concerned as earlier African-American women writers with her audience's misperception of her characters as "primitive," yet a similar tension between the codes of white and black female sexuality persists in her fiction. Her story "Advancing Luna—and Ida B. Wells," Barbara Christian points out, "focuses on the convoluted connection between rape and lynchings, sex and race, that continues to this day" (469). Unlike Helga Crane, Walker's protagonist assumes that it is white society that is sexually perverse and that interracial rape *always* occurs between white men and black women. In the black community at least, black women are no longer seen as complicitous. At first she is shocked when her white friend reveals that she has been raped by a black man. Eventually she feels angry and betrayed by Luna because she realizes that her friend, despite her decision not to use it, maintains the power to cry "rape" and threaten the security of the black community.

The author was never able to finish this story to her satisfaction (the version in *You Can't Keep a Good Woman Down* contains "Second Thoughts," "Imaginary Knowledge," and a "Postscript"), reflecting her own ambivalence about the ability of white and black women to overcome the divisions between women caused by racism, and her uncertain stance continues in *The Color Purple*. Her decision to isolate Celie's self-development in the black community suggests how difficult it might be for her protagonist to overcome sexual oppression and realize her own identity given the additional factor of racial oppression. Like Janie, she can fight only one obstacle at a time. Both successfully "get man off [their] eyeball" but must reject heterosexuality in order to do so. They can hardly have excess energy to battle the larger world of racism.

The earlier *Meridian*, in fact, comes closer to resolving the constricting stereotypes of black and white female sexuality. At least there is dialogue and forgiveness between Meridian and Lynne once they recognize and understand each other's suffering (181). In *The Color Purple*, however, Walker is more doubtful. White women like Miz Millie and even her daughter Eleanor Jane learn too slowly how their presence threatens the black community. Their privileged status still depends upon the oppression of others; consequently, they remain allied with the patriarchal system. The next chapter discusses Sherley Williams's *Dessa Rose*, a pastoral which, through recasting a historical incident from the antebellum past, imagines a way for black *and* white women to cross over the barriers of race and privilege together.

6. Sherley Williams's Post-Pastoral Vision: *Dessa Rose*

> This novel, then, is fiction; all the characters, even the country they travel through, while based on fact, are inventions. And what is here is as true as if I myself had lived it. Maybe it is only a metaphor, but I now own a summer in the 19th century. And this is for the children . . . who will share in the 21st.
>
> —Sherley Williams, Author's Note, *Dessa Rose*

Dessa Rose, the poet Sherley Anne Williams's first novel, imagines a different world from Alice Walker's *The Color Purple*. While *The Color Purple* recasts the populist myth of the black folk, *Dessa Rose* reworks the patriarchal tradition through its use of a historical antebellum setting and adoption of slave-narrative conventions. For black writers, the antebellum society was not a place to memorialize or recreate imaginatively. After Charles Chesnutt's ironic pastoral romances, and until the 1970s, few twentieth-century African-American novelists have attempted to explore the plantation world as a means of questioning or countering white versions of this genre.[1] Black pastorals of the 1920s through the 1950s focused instead on the city-versus-country schematic: the rural South could be idealized only once it was left behind for the urban North. Robert Bone explains that pastorals of the Harlem Renaissance period were "rooted in the deepest emotional needs of the Negro masses. Nostalgia for the rural South was strong among the black migrants, as the blues tradition will attest. Disenchantment with the Promised Land was equally intense, and it produced a sharp emotional revulsion from city values and city ways" (133).

And, according to Barbara Christian, African-American women writers also waited before returning to the landscape of a painful past. Starting in the 1970s, Christian notes, black women authors began examining their mothers' lives in the 1920s through the 1940s with novels like Toni Morrison's *The Bluest Eye* (1970) and Alice Walker's *The Third Life of Grange Copeland* (1970). Black women writers have begun to return to their great grandmothers' stories only recently (Christian, "Somebody Forgot to Tell Somebody Something"). Margaret Walker's *Jubilee* (1966), the story of her slave ancestor Vyry, is an exception to this trend, or perhaps rather a precursor to a new phase of historical fiction treating the antebellum and reconstruction South. *Dessa Rose,* then, revives African-American interest in the southern past by imagining an antebellum setting.

Because *Dessa Rose* might be loosely categorized as "plantation fiction," at first it appears to resemble Willa Cather's anti-plantation romance, *Sapphira and the Slave Girl,* or even Margaret Mitchell's *Gone with the Wind* more than it does most contemporary African-American fiction.[2] Like Cather and Mitchell, Williams begins by dismantling the southern pastoral world and questioning the archetype of the southern garden. The three novels also pose significant questions about the possibility of interracial understanding and community among women. Like Alice Walker, though in an antebellum context, Williams directly focuses on the dual problems of sexism and racism. *Dessa Rose* takes the confrontation between black and white women one step further than *The Color Purple* by imagining not only the possibility of mutual understanding (as with Sofia and Eleanor Jane), but also friendship.

Dessa Rose responds more directly to a slave-narrative tradition than does Walker and the earlier white women authors of the southern pastoral. Its representation of the southern plantation, as in Margaret Walker's *Jubilee* (1966) and Alex Haley's *Roots* (1976), draws on conventions inherited from nineteenth-century autobiographies of ex-slaves—including the slave auction, the cruel treatment of slaves by an evil master, and the miraculous escape.[3] But it also parodies these plot devices, not only to particularize Dessa's story, but to reclaim it as a black *woman's* story. Jean Yellin has emphasized the importance of authenticating the few extant slave narratives by African-American women with her work validating Harriet Jacobs's *Incidents in the Life of a Slave Girl* (1861). Jacobs' narrative, Yellin explains, differs in many respects from the prototypical male narrative. Jacobs addresses all American women, black and white, in an unconventional call for sisterhood and defies taboos about discussing female sexuality.[4] More than a century later, Williams's narrative of a female slave is presented from the same perspective. The novel at once empowers the black female voice and challenges negative assumptions about interracial bonding among women.

As Deborah McDowell points out, because slave narratives were mostly written by and about black men, black women, both pre– and post–Civil War, have had to revise these plots through a fictional format. Accordingly, more contemporary novels about slavery have been written by African-American women. These fictional narratives are important because, as McDowell argues, they "posit a female-gendered subjectivity, more complex in dimension, that dramatize[s] not what was *done* to slave women, but what they *did* with what was done to them" ("Negotiating Between Tenses" 146). A fictional slave narrative further gives the author control over her own text; rather than legitimizing her story with testimonials and introductions by white supporters, she could introduce her own narrative and explain its purpose.

Following the example of early twentieth-century African-American women writers, Williams begins *Dessa Rose* with an "Author's Note" to explain her use of historical slave accounts. In 1899, Pauline Hopkins felt it necessary to explain her reasons for writing a fictionalized account of black history: "I have presented both sides of the dark picture—lynching and concubinage—truthfully and without vituperation, pleading for that justice of heart

and mind for my people . . ." (15). A century later, Williams's justi–
fication need not be as defensive. Unlike earlier actual and fictional
slave narratives, *Dessa Rose* does not purport to address a white
abolitionist audience. Instead, it is framed in the epilogue as
Dessa's oral retelling of her own experience to her son and grandchildren.

Perhaps the most noticeable convention of the slave narrative
the novel revises is the narrator. Rather than privileging a white
sponsor or as-told-to recorder of the story, the novel undercuts the
white male voice. Adam Nehemiah's attempt to appropriate Dessa's
"confession" into an examination of what he calls the "origins of
uprisings among slaves" (17) fails miserably.[5] Aside from his unwill–
ingness to listen to her version of events, he literally cannot keep
her in captivity long enough to record the story—she escapes with
her body and her narrative intact. We can see Williams's displacement of Nehemiah even more clearly by comparing the novel to
the author's earlier short story version, "Meditations on History,"
which appeared in Mary Washington's collection *Midnight Birds*
(1980). Most of the earlier draft is devoted to Nehemiah's journal,
and the drama of the story occurs with Dessa's disappearance and
the subsequent silencing of Nehemiah at the end. The novel continues the plot essentially where the story stops—with the life of
Dessa as a fugitive.

As the novel progresses, less and less space is devoted to
Nehemiah's journal reflections, and his final appearance in the
last section when he tries to recapture Dessa completely undermines his authority and credibility. In the sheriff's office, Dessa
stares at the now disheveled Nehemiah and reflects: "Now, I
thought, now his shirt don't even have no collar; his ankles dirty.
My eyes filled with tears then. To be brought so low by such a
trifling white man. This what chance will do, children, trample
over all your dreams, swing a bony ankle in front of you" (247).
His presence is no longer threatening to her because he does not
fit the code of "respectability" in white society. Finally, his story is

literally undone as well. Rufel's baby Clara knocks his journal out of his hands, "[t]he pages wasn't bound in the cover and they fell out, scattering about the floor." The sheriff can detect nothing but scribbling on them (255). Dessa can now finish telling her own story.

What is important for this study, however, is not how the novel rewrites and subverts the slave-narrative genre but how it both departs from and appropriates aspects of the southern pastoral in order to create a new "post-pastoral" vision. Nehemiah's journal/ narrative, in this sense, represents the traditional male "pastoral impulse." As a specious "Adam," he views land, the southern garden, as something to be exploited to gain power. Realizing that "land, not learning, was the entrée to planter society" (18), he determines to win literary fame—money—so that he can purchase his entrance into the aristocracy. His journey through the South to capture Dessa is an attempt to claim woman as property, ironically like the planters' appropriation of the white southern lady for the same end.

Just as Nehemiah's view is discredited, however, the plot also reverses plantation-fiction conventions at textual and figurative levels. First, it concerns not reconciliation between North and South or new and old orders of white society but imagines instead a moment of intersection between the white and black worlds, freedom and bondage. The plantation mistress, "Miz Rufel," has been abandoned by her husband, and no gallant southern gentleman appears on the scene to assume the hero's role. Aside from Nehemiah, no white male figures take significant roles in the plot. The absence of men threatens the intact patriarchal structure and allows the development of a different kind of plantation community.

This new community, composed of a lone white woman and a group of runaway slaves, recognizes no race hierarchy in relationships. Despite her privileged status, Rufel is as trapped as the runaways, for she has no knowledge of farming or management.

Her absent husband holds the title to the land. As long as the escaped slaves remain on the plantation, they share with Rufel the same freedom from the codes of a patriarchal slave society. Not a miniature of the larger world, the plantation in Williams's novel presents an alternative to it. No one owns the land since the white master has disappeared. In fact, the "plantation" is really just a stage set. The big house's second story, Rufel reflects, was "still no more than a Georgian front and an empty, slant-roofed shell, the kitchen barely a lean-to covering that monstrous cook-stove" (113).

In Section II, "The Wench," the runaways gradually educate Rufel about the gruesome realities of slavery—of using people as property—making her recognize and finally reject the plantation system.[6] This recognition can come only after she has abandoned the role of plantation mistress in a series of painful confrontations with the runaways. First, even before Dessa's arrival, she learns how as a white aristocratic woman she has been sheltered from (or denied) the truth about master/slave relations. Doubting that Ada could have been so mistreated by a "cruel master" who tries to seduce her daughter, Rufel tells her mammy, "No white man would do that. . ." and is silenced by her with the retort, "men can do things a *lady* can't even guess at" (94). Rufel had never considered that miscegenation was actually the sexual abuse of black women, not the exoticism of a mulatto mistress. But she is not yet prepared to believe Dessa's story or accept the new arrivals' refusal to treat her with deference.

It shocks her to find Dessa's eyes glaring at her in fear and loathing merely because of her white skin. She thinks, "never, never had [she] done anything to anyone to deserve such a look. But to see eyes so like Mammy's, staring such hatred at her. It had given Rufel quite a turn. She wanted the girl to wake up, wanted to see that look banished from her face" (101). Rufel still believes she can command "darkies" to do her bidding. She does not realize that, just as she regards all blacks as her "servants," without considering their humanity, so they also might look upon her not as an individual woman but as a representative of a racist system.

Nowhere is Rufel's ignorance about her racist attitudes more apparent than in her relationship with her "mammy," whom she had loved selfishly, as a child would, depending on her for every physical and emotional need. She had never considered that her slave had any life outside of gratifying the mistress's wants.[7] Dessa, furious that Rufel could co-opt her memories of her own mammy, finally confronts her:

> "Your 'mammy'!" No *white* girl could ever have taken *her* place in mammy's bosom; no one. "You ain't go no 'mammy,' . . . All you know about is this kinda sleeve and that kinda bonnet; some party here—Didn't you have no peoples where you lived? 'Mammy' ain't nobody name, not they real one." (125)

Unable to recall her mammy's real name or whether she had any children, Rufel is forced to admit to herself that she never really knew her "mammy," never understood her. In a moment of insight, Rufel comes to realize the depth of her ignorance: "Almost she felt personally responsible for Mammy's pain, personally connected to it, not as the soother of hurt as Mammy had always been for her, but as the source of that pain. . . . And Mammy—Had anyone ever whipped her?" (147–48). Dessa challenges Rufel to rethink her relationship, not only with Dorcas (her "mammy") but with all those whom she has—however unknowingly—oppressed through her role as plantation mistress. After this painful recognition, Rufel can now participate as an equal member in the new farm community. She begins to see herself, not as superior, but as a co-worker in a cooperative venture.

Williams transforms the plantation using the populist myth of the independent or yeoman farm. Each worker takes responsibility for some part of its operation. Harker, with his knowledge of farming methods, oversees the crop production. Ada runs the household, and Nathan provides meat and fish with his hunting and trapping. Even before she has rejected her role as plantation mistress, Rufel learns to fill in where needed. Taking Dessa's newborn baby to her breast, she reflects, ". . . she was a little crazy, she supposed. But she could do something about this, about the baby who continued to cry. . . . She—Rufel—could do something. That was as close as she came to explaining anything to herself. The baby was hungry and she fed him" (98). Symbolically, this action, though she is unconscious of its consequences at this point, marks Rufel's entry into the new community. Like her literary predecessors from Dorinda to Celie, Rufel learns the value of productive work.

Of course, like the women's community at Merry Hill in *The Dollmaker* and Cather's communal vision at the end of *Sapphira and the Slave Girl*, Williams's egalitarian farm community is temporary and created out of special circumstances. It must establish its own code of operation and behavior. According to Nina Auerbach, such a "code seems a whispered and a fleeting thing, more a buried language than a rallying cry" (8). The plantation in *Dessa Rose* is not self-sufficient but rather a makeshift means of survival for outcasts. Its main value is to provide a way for a disparate group of people to learn to work together and trust one another before they depart on their slave-selling ruse. Race and gender present the two barriers that must be crossed first. Again, as in the earlier female pastorals, farming becomes the means by which new relationships among characters can be established. Once property relations are transformed, character interactions also change.

Farming or closeness to nature in the female southern pastoral enables harmonious relationships between men and women. Like Glasgow's Ada and Ralph in *Vein of Iron*, who escape to Thunder Mountain to celebrate their union, Dessa and Harker consecrate their love outside, under the trees. Harker tells her, "I don't want to love you in the woods cause we don't have no place else to be" (209). Sexual passion can be expressed freely once the lovers leave societal censure behind. Dessa and Harker's love, like Rufel and Nathan's interracial union, would have been impossible in the larger slaveholding world where blacks are recognized as "property," not people.

Significantly, in *Dessa Rose*, it is the black men who become "naturalized" characters rather than the women. Dessa's first lover Kaine, in fact, is described much as black "earth mother" figures are in earlier plantation fiction: ". . . his voice high and clear as running water over a settled stream bed . . ." (1), and "[h]is lips . . . firm and velvety as the tip of a cat-tail willow" (4). Both Kaine and Harker are seen from Dessa's eyes: "Kaine was like sunshine; like song. Harker was thunder and lightening" (209). Connecting black men with nature simultaneously frees the female protagonist from her automatic association with fertility and underlines the mutual objectification of male and female slaves.

This objectification is revealed in Nathan's exploitation by his white mistress for her sexual gratification. Some time later, Nathan finally realizes why his mistress took slave lovers: "If she had tried to satisfy her sexual needs with white men, even ones outside her own class, she would have had no way of ensuring their silence. If a black man boasted, she could have his life. . . . This is what Miz Lorraine wanted: to be in control" (169–70). Male and female slaves are subject to their owners' absolute authority over their bodies. Miz Lorraine acts out of both power and fear in this case. As a woman she remains vulnerable to the same sexual exploitation to which she exposes Nathan; her desire for control over her own body results in her using her slave's.

Although Rufel does not "own" Nathan, her status as a white woman makes their sexual relationship suspect. Is Rufel attracted to him as a sexual object like his former mistress? Or does Nathan deliberately seduce Rufel in order to convince her to join the slave-selling scheme as is suggested by a conversation Dessa overhears between Harker and Cully (179)? Williams, I believe, is purposely unclear about the motives for this relationship. It is too easy for readers to draw simplistic conclusions about miscegenation. At

least initially, the reader learns, Rufel "used [Nathan] much as she
had Mammy, as the means through which she participated in the
life beyond the yard" (158). But just as her relationship to Dorcas
is both loving and exploitative, her involvement with Nathan is
equally paradoxical. *Dessa Rose* shows the double threat behind
such a relationship. First, it threatens the white paternalistic system which depends upon separation of white women and black
men to ensure racially pure family lines and perpetuate the need
for white male "protection" of white women's "virtue."[8] Second,
and just as important, Nathan's involvement with Rufel strains the
already uneasy bonds between black men and women. The women
worry that it puts the whole community in danger; they realize
that "[w]hite mens would kill to keep something like this quiet"
(190).

However, it is Dessa who feels most betrayed by Nathan's "lay-
ing up" at the "big house." Rufel has interfered with the unusual
friendship she and Nathan had shared since they escaped from
the coffle together. As in *The Color Purple*, understanding between
oppressed men and women is not automatic even though they
bear similar burdens. Black women are subject to a double oppression—from their white masters and from black men who accept
the whites' dehumanization of them. Arguing over Nathan's and
Rufel's sexual involvement, the fugitives turn against one another.
Ned tells Janet that she is jealous "cause [Nathan] not diddling
her" and accuses her of being "an old mule" (198).[9] Dessa's reaction to this is hurt and anger:

> Was this what they thought of us? Mules. I was so choked I couldn't
> speak. I used to warm my feet against Kaine's legs in winter; time
> they got me out that cellar, my heels was so rough they snagged a
> tear in them sheets up to the House . . . . But Ned wasn't talking
> about no color, no feel. . . . Janet was mistreated cause she was
> barren; Ada's master had belly-rubbed with her, then wanted to
> use her daughter. I had been spared death till I could birth a baby
> white folks would keep slaved. Oh, we was mules all right. What

else would peoples use like they used us? . . . Had he really wanted
me to be like Mistress, I wondered, like Miz Ruint, that doughy
skin and slippery hair? Was *that* what they wanted? (198–99)

What Ned is "talking about" is the difficulty of black men and
women understanding each other's pain, especially when the white
mistress is used as a standard of sexual attractiveness.

Dessa and Nathan eventually recover their friendship in a
poignant, painful scene after they have witnessed a slave auction.
Nathan runs after Dessa to comfort her, and she accepts his embrace spontaneously, for a moment forgetting her anger toward
him. Significantly, it is he who forces the confrontation between
them. As Dessa later retells the scene:

Till then, he would keep at me: Say "friend," say "brother." And
whether I said yes or no to him, it wouldn't never be the way it
used to be. I guess this was always my pain, that things would never
be the same. I had lost so much, so much, and this brother was a
part of what I'd gained. Nathan—he wasn't grinning then. No, he
held my hand and looked at me steady on. . . . (224)

What is important about this reconciliation is that the two agree to
respect each other's differences. They can be friends without sharing the same viewpoints. Williams's pastoral presents a fully realized friendship between a male and a female character. Unlike her
predecessors Glasgow, Mitchell, Cather, Arnow and Walker, she
has found the dialogue to enact a crucial moment of understanding.

Another relationship more fully realized in *Dessa Rose* than in
the previous female pastorals is the friendship that develops between Dessa and Rufel, a black and a white woman. In the other
pastorals, interracial female friendship is absent or emblematic as
in Gertie Nevels's encounter with the "brown woman" on the train
to Detroit in *The Dollmaker.* In Williams's novel, however, this encounter becomes the focal point of the plot. Dessa and Rufel must
shed their mutual misconceptions in order to participate in a *new*

southern garden. This process had begun over the naming of "mammy" in Section II. As Deborah McDowell notes, physical intimacy between the two women is established before their emotional bond develops (151–53). They sleep together in the big house while Dessa is recovering from childbirth, and Rufel becomes wet nurse for Dessa's baby. On the plantation, nonetheless, neither is able to overcome her suspicions about the other. Rufel does not believe Dessa's story about her beating, and even when she inadvertently witnesses Dessa undressing and sees her loins, "like a mutilated cat face," she cannot find the words to express her sympathy (166–67).

Only when they are on the road and experience the same danger and fear are the two women able to overcome the resentment between them. This occurs one night on a plantation they visit when the white planter tries to rape Rufel. She calls on Dessa to help push him out of her bed, and after attacking and driving him away with pillows, the two collapse in laughter and relief. This moment is strangely reminiscent of Scarlett and Melanie's confrontation with the Union soldier in *Gone with the Wind.* United by a common purpose, the women act out the bond they are unable to articulate. In *Dessa Rose*, however, Dessa and Rufel not only become conscious of the possibility and value of friendship but also gradually learn to express it. After the attempted rape, Dessa realizes:

> I hadn't knowed white mens could use a white woman like, just take her by force same as could with us. . . . I never will forget the fear that come on me when Miz Lady called me on Mr. Oscar, that *knowing* that she was as helpless in this as I was, that our only protection was ourselfs and each others. (220)

Although this incident teaches Dessa compassion for Rufel and links them closer together through shared oppression, they do not yet completely trust each other. Dessa never forgets that Rufel can always exercise more privilege and freedom than she.

Rufel can never know what it is like to be a slave, and Dessa avoids telling her about the pain she feels over losing her lover Kaine: "So we didn't talk too much that was personal. I mean, I know I mentioned mammy-nem, and she talked about Dorcas. . . . But this was a white woman and I don't think I forgot it that whole, entire journey" (237).

True friendship develops only at the very end of the novel before the two women part forever. Rufel, with the help of another slave woman who testifies falsely about Dessa's identity, saves Dessa from being recaptured by Nehemiah.[10] At last they find the words to express their feelings for each other; significantly they call each other by their real names, "Dessa" and "Ruth." Wanting to hug Ruth, Dessa must be content to hug her daughter Clara in public: "We couldn't hug each other, not on the streets, not in Arcopolis, not even after dark," she relates, "but that night we walked the boardwalk together and we didn't hide our grins" (256).

Although the world of the antebellum South forbids this relationship, Williams can imagine it outside the boundaries of historical reality. This is, perhaps, the most important consequence of the southern female pastoral, its transcendence of the codes of an oppressive society and its creation of new relationships that overcome racial and sexual barriers. *Dessa Rose*, in this sense, moves beyond the pastoral framework of the other five novels examined in this study. It is a "post-" pastoral because the characters' interactions with the land become secondary to the new community envisioned. Although Rufel and the others begin to work out an egalitarian society on the plantation, actual fellowship occurs only after they leave the southern garden behind. Perhaps it is too reminiscent of the past, and only out west can they start anew.

During the slave-selling scheme, we are given a glimpse of the kind of interracial, cooperative community the runaways and Rufel might have been able to establish had they all journeyed west together. After each successful scam, they pause to tell stories and laugh together. Dessa reflects that even the pairs of lovers lose significance compared to the group's cohesion: "And after a while, we was too close to hold hands, if you know what I mean, too mindful about everybody to show much that was special to one person" (225).

Regardless of the intimacy and understanding the runaways and Rufel establish, the novel ends with dissolution of this new community. The post-pastoral vision of *Dessa Rose*, as in the other female pastorals, cannot finally be sustained. Female agrarian heroes like Dorinda triumph alone, or like Scarlett and Sapphira through exploiting the code of white supremacy. Those women protagonists who participate in new communities—like Gertie, Rachel, and Celie—must do so outside the boundaries of recognized society; consequently, the values they express are always threatened. Despite the fragility of this vision, these pastorals function, I believe, as predictors of new roles and relationships in southern society, particularly for women.

In a recent talk entitled "History as Prophecy: *Dessa Rose* and *Beloved*," Cora Kaplan discussed the "two spaces of memory" in contemporary historical novels by black women, historiographic time and psychic time. The latter, she claims, is offered as an oblique critique of the way the history of slavery has been posed by black men. But, I argue, African-American women novelists rewrite history, not only to correct it, but also to create a place for themselves in aesthetic and political discourse. Neither *Dessa Rose* nor *Beloved* is a thoroughly researched document, for each freely interprets historical incident to imagine an alternative possibility, a way of healing the wounds of slavery. Recent southern historians confirm that sisterhood between black and white women was at best a rare occurrence before and after the Civil War.[11] In this sense, *Dessa Rose* is more a utopian than a realistic vision.

However, as Annette Kolodny has emphasized with the archetype of the American landscape, in order for changed attitudes toward and by women to occur, we must first be able to imagine new relationships; so the world of slavery might be recast to project a future of interracial understanding. Curiously, of the six female pastorals discussed, *Dessa Rose* has perhaps the most in common with what might initially appear to be its antithesis, *Gone with the Wind.* Both use historical settings as backdrops to examine contemporary issues. *GWTW* prophesies different gender roles while Williams's novel explores new racial relationships. In each, the plantation becomes a locus for experimenting with new ways for men and women to interact. Scarlett and Will Benteen can communicate through their mutual devotion to the land, and Rufel and Nathan can realize their love without being condemned for miscegenation. Female friendship, while problematic, becomes the pivotal point of the plot—Scarlett is devastated more by Melanie's death than by the loss of Rhett's love, and Dessa dwells on her memory of her unusual bond with Rufel as she retells her experience to her grandchildren.

Williams's reshaping of the plantation myth, nonetheless, is more conscious than Mitchell's. She once explained in an interview: "For me writing is a process of ordering the world. It is a process of bringing insight, playing around with possibilities, solutions, in a way I could never play around with actual life" (Claudia Tate 211). *Dessa Rose,* I believe, is a testament to that process. And, in a sense, Williams's statement expresses the aim of female pastoral—to envision a new southern garden where men and women, blacks and whites, can live and work side by side.

Epilogue

Female pastoral, as I have defined it, is a transitory genre; it is a vehicle through which women writers have challenged stereotypes and envisioned, not only new relationships among characters, but changing class interactions. Unlike the southern agrarians of the 1920s and 30s, the six authors I have examined urge a radical restructuring of society rather than a return to traditional rural values. Curiously, for both, pastoral is a means of displacement for class mobility occurring during periods of urbanization. But while the agrarians and other male pastoralists like William Faulkner resist change through nostalgic evocation of the past, the women authors of this study respond to the same or similar phenomena by experimenting with gender roles and re-imagining property relationships. Ellen Glasgow and Margaret Mitchell explore female autonomy in rural settings. Harriette Arnow and Alice Walker focus on female identity and friendship by drawing on a muse from nature. Willa Cather and Sherley Williams use the antebellum plantation as a locus for reexamining interracial relationships. That the white authors of this study are less able to envision racial equality among characters reflects the reality of a segregated South before 1955.

Contemporary women authors writing about the American South seem less likely to turn to pastoral since the country's transformation from a rural to an urban society is almost complete. Bobbie Ann Mason's Kentucky landscapes are covered with K-marts and parking garages, and at the end of Lee Smith's *Oral History*, the ancestral Hoot Owl Holler becomes the site of a theme park. Neither author depicts a woman protagonist as empowered by her relationship to the land. African-American writers continue to use female pastoral in historical novels; Gloria Naylor's *Mama Day* is one example. Unlike white authors, African-American women continue to associate female strength and identity with a bond to nature.

Whether both white and black women writers will abandon female pastoral as an unecessary displacement of gender, race, and class conflict remains uncertain. What seems clear is that the restructuring of the archetype of American landscape is enabling a new generation of writers—women and men—to challenge restrictive myths and mores of American society.

Notes

Preface

1. Louise Westling's *Sacred Groves and Ravaged Gardens: The Fiction of Eudora Welty, Carson McCullers, and Flannery O'Connor* examines the fiction of three southern women authors with some discussion of the relationship of women and the land, and Minrose Gwin discusses Margaret Walker's vision of community in *Jubilee* in *Black and White Women of the Old South: The Peculiar Sisterhood in American Literature*.

2. In "What Was Penelope Unweaving," Heilbrun explains the limitations on woman's story: "In literature and out, through all recorded history, women have lived by a script they did not write. Their destiny was to be married, circulated; to be given by one man, the father, to another, the husband; to become the mothers of men. Theirs has been the marriage plot, the erotic plot, the courtship plot, but never, as for men, the quest plot" (108).

Introduction

1. Two relevant studies of the political and class dimensions of pastoral literature are William Empson, *Some Versions of Pastoral* (1935), and Raymond Williams, *The Country and the City* (1973).

2. Cash's *The Mind of the South* (1941) is perhaps the most widely known critique of southern culture and history. For more recent discussions of the myth see works by Gray, King, MacKethan, and Singal.

3. On Kennedy see Werner, "The Old South, 1815–1840" in Rubin et al., *The History of Southern Literature* 90–91.

4. Bargainner, Buck, Lentz, and Ridgely discuss the development of the postbellum plantation romance tradition. Buck's *Road to Reunion* chapter 8, in particular, examines the function of reunion marriages between southern and northern protagonists. See also MacKethan, "Plantation Fiction, 1865–1900," in Rubin et al. 209–18.

5. See Mixon, "Humor, Romance and Realism" in Rubin et al. 246–51.

6. See Chesnutt's *The Colonel's Dream* (1905), in particular, which dispels racial myths through its ironic use of pastoral conventions.

7. King discusses his "Southern Renaissance" in a Freudian context, using the "family romance" to define the pastoral as the struggle between father and son in such works as William Faulkner's *Go Down, Moses* and Robert Penn Warren's *All the King's Men.* The only woman he includes is Lillian Smith, about whom he speculates that her "ersatz mother role as camp director and her insistence upon the importance of the body was a way of redirecting her unfilled desires" (190). Other white women authors are not considered because "they were not concerned primarily with larger cultural, racial, and political themes" (9), and African-American writers "are not taken up because for them the Southern family romance was hardly problematic. It could be and was rejected out of hand" (8).

   Simpson identifies a broader canon of southern authors, but like King, he asserts that the major theme of the period is "a recovery—a restoration, perhaps a reconstruction—of memory and history" (70). Fiction of the renaissance, he claims, is no "sociological plea" (78) but rather "an effort to achieve a vision of the meaning of the South in terms of the classical-Christian historical order of being . . ." (75).

8. See Woodward, *The Burden of Southern History,* especially chapter 1, "The Search for Southern Identity," in which he discusses the multiple "Lost Causes," i.e., events that shook the South's self-consciousness. He defines agrarianism as a second lost cause and segregation as a possible third (12). See also Scott's discussion of the effects of women's suffrage on the South in *The Southern Lady,* especially chapters 8 and 9 (186–231). She concludes: "The

Nineteenth Amendment changed a good many things, but it only partially modified southern culture. A number of difficulties remained in the way of women's full participation in public life. One major obstacle, in addition to the demands of home and family, was widespread male opposition, typified, perhaps, by the Texan who burned his wife's poll tax receipt to prevent her from voting" (209).

9. Tate's novel implicitly develops tenets in his agrarian philosophy first expounded in *I'll Take My Stand*, a radical, reactionary manifesto written by twelve southerners at Vanderbilt University in 1930. The agrarians began an attack on industrialized society—the North—which they viewed as a threat to the southern agricultural economy. They championed the yeoman farmer ideal proposed by Thomas Jefferson in the eighteenth century. Key to the rural society they envisioned was a continued paternalistic attitude toward blacks—farm labor—as well as an insistence on a patriarchal order. See Conkin, *The South in Southern Agrarianism* (133–39).

10. See, for instance, Thadious Davis, "Some Standard Bearers in the New Negro Renaissance" (Rubin et al. 291–313). She observes that "Toomer was the quintessential voice of the black Southern artist heralding a new consciousness of black life and a reinterpretation of the South for that life" (298). Bell and Mootry refute this interpretation of Toomer as unequivocal rural spokesperson.

11. See Gilbert and Gubar's pioneering study of the female imagination, *The Madwoman in the Attic: The Woman Writer and the Nineteenth Century Literary Imagination*, especially chapter 1, "The Queen's Looking Glass: Female Creativity, Male Images of Women and the Metaphor of Literary Paternity." The authors explain: "For all literary artists, of course, self-definition necessarily precedes self-assertion: the creative 'I am' cannot be uttered if the 'I' knows not what it is. But for the female artist the essential process of self-definition is complicated by all those patriarchal definitions that intervene between herself and herself" (17).

12. Glasgow depicts hostile nature, in *Barren Ground* (1925) represented as broomsedge, as a force over which the female hero

must triumph or control. Black women writers from Hurston onwards evoke the wrathful power of nature (such as storms, floods, etc.) in order to present an almost animistic force. See Gloria Naylor's *Mama Day* (1988) for recent use of this imagery.

13. See Sylvia Cook, *From Tobacco Road to Route 66*, especially chapter 1, "The Development of the Poor White Tradition" (3–17). For a discussion of the simultaneous development of the patriarchal/plantation myth and the populist/yeoman farmer myth see Richard Gray, *Writing the South*. Gray views Jefferson as the originator of the yeoman farmer ideal and William Randolph as anticipating the patriarchal myth (1–30).

Chapter 1

1. Many critics dwell on Glasgow's rejection of the southern belle but do not consider her revision of genre as well as character conventions. See, for instance, Jones (*Tomorrow Is Another Day* 225–70), Kreyling (76–102) and Seidel (74–96). By "naturalistic" I mean the school of American fiction in the early twentieth century followed by Norris, Crane, Dreiser, and others in which nature is depicted as an overwhelming, deterministic force. Glasgow and other women writers of this period viewed nature differently from their male counterparts. Nancy Walker argues that Glasgow, Chopin, and Wharton imposed limitations on their female protagonists more from societal and personal influences than from cosmic forces (143–45). I believe Glasgow depicts nature's omnipotence through her characters' "misreading" of its signs. See Raper (*Without Shelter*) for the influence of Darwin and evolutionary theory on the author's work.

2. Gray ("Writing the South," 101–2) and Hardy discuss Glasgow's class concerns and rural reform measures, but neither considers how these issues affect either her characterization of women or her challenge to the mythic substructure of the southern pastoral.

3. Although Glasgow's earlier novels—like *The Descendant* (1897), in which the protagonist, Michael Akershem, comes from a poor white background—concern the lower classes, they do not develop

realistic psychological portrayals of the characters. Akershem's relationships with other characters appear particularly shallow compared to the friendship between Dan and Pinetop in *The Battle-Ground*.

4. See Raper's discussion of the cycles of nature in *The Deliverance* (*Without Shelter* 184–99). In Glasgow's later novels, *Barren Ground* and *Vein of Iron*, autumn becomes a time of fruition for the female protagonist. Here, however, the reverse is true: lovers do not typically unite in autumn.

5. Recent studies of Glasgow reexamine her critique of southern society but underrate the author's early experimentation with gender roles. Watson believes that *The Battle-Ground* lies wholly within the sentimental tradition (235). Kreyling, likewise, dates Glasgow's departure from the "patriarchal fortress" of southern romantic writing with her novel *Life and Gabriella* (95–96). Glasgow's short stories, most of which were written after the publication of *Life and Gabriella* and before *Barren Ground*, perhaps represent her final death knell to the southern plantation tradition. Many of these are ghost stories picturing the grotesque world of an effete aristocracy. See, for instance, "Jordan's End."

6. Few critics consider *Barren Ground* as part of the southern pastoral tradition. Raper discusses its natural imagery as representative of Dorinda's desire for revenge (*From the Sunken Garden* 79–100), and Wagner groups the novel with *Vein of Iron* and *Virginia* as a study of female character (118). Hardy's chapter on Glasgow in Rubin and Jacob's *Southern Renascence* (1953) labels *Barren Ground* and *The Miller of Old Church* as pastorals but sees them as "a quest for realism" (242). Gray notes Glasgow's agrarian agenda and observes that ". . . in the best of her heroic novels, Glasgow managed to go beyond the accepted to encompass an almost mystical belief in the efficacy of direct contact with the earth" ("The Literature of Memory,"29). Bond uses the term "pastoral" to compare the novel with classical rather than American motifs (567–68). None of these critics recognizes the author's revision of the southern pastoral myth.

7. The embedded captivity narratives in this novel nonetheless conform, for the most part, to the negative stereotype of the Native

American although the Indians' "wildness" is a positive trait acquired by Ada's ancestor Martha Tod.

8. Compare this scene with William Gilmore Simms' *The Yemassee.* William Faulkner's portrayal of Indians, especially in *Go Down, Moses* relates women and land exploitation as well. In "Delta Autumn" both land and woman are violated by white men; only the Indians understand that nature cannot be *owned.* In chapter 2, I discuss how Margaret Mitchell uses this imagery of captivity narratives to depict Scarlett O'Hara's female ancestors.

9. Diony Hall, the novel's female hero, nonetheless differs from the male pattern. As Kolodny discusses in *The Land Before Her,* women's fantasies about the frontier involved cultivating gardens rather than conquering the wilderness. Accordingly, Diony tells Daniel Boone who tells her that he never feels lost even in unfamiliar territory, "I'm not the Boone kind. . . . I'd be more at home somewheres else" (186).

10. Compare Glasgow's Ada with Hurston's Janie in *Their Eyes Were Watching God* (1937). Janie and Ada both develop and express their sexuality through nature (Janie's sexual awakening occurs in a beautiful scene as she watches a bee fertilize a blossom from a pear tree), and both are in a sense "punished" for their sexual awakening. Ada loses Ralph's faithfulness, and Janie is forced to kill her lover Tea Cake in order to save her own life.

11. Glasgow's last two novels, *In This Our Life* (1941) and *Beyond Defeat* (incomplete and published posthumously in 1966), continue the quest for communal values and a more harmonious relationship between men and women through shared work in a rural environment. Kate Oliver inherits Dorinda's role as autonomous female farmer, yet her story is not central to the plot. Again, as in *Vein,* it is the older man, in this case Asa Timberlake, who recognizes the restorative properties of tilling the earth. Asa's and Kate's friendship recasts that between Dorinda and Nathan— romantic love is replaced by mutual respect.

12. This story has recently been reprinted in *Ellen Glasgow's Reasonable Doubts: A Collection of Her Writings,* ed. Julius Rowan Raper.

Chapter 2

1. See Irvin's article "Gea in Georgia: A Mythic Dimension in *Gone with the Wind*," in which Scarlett is analyzed as the daughter of Gea, the Earth Mother goddess of classical antiquity. While Irvin does consider the protagonist's metaphoric connection to the landscape, she does not examine it in the context of the mythic *southern* garden.

2. Malcolm Cowley was the first to label the novel "an encyclopedia of the plantation legend." See Harwell, which excerpts Cowley's 1936 review of the novel in *The New Republic* (66n). In "Scarlett O'Hara and the Two Quentin Compsons," Louis D. Rubin, Jr., compares Scarlett to Faulkner's Thomas Sutpen in *Absalom, Absalom!* and examines the two characters' similar ambitions to recreate a "design" of the past. Gender roles are not an important issue for either critic.

3. Seidel argues that Scarlett, as well, is such a southern belle and "is trapped by a code that has created her narcissism and prevented her from accepting her own sexual passion" (57). I believe, however, that Scarlett rejects this code from the outset despite her specious observance of it.

4. Faulkner and some others of Mitchell's contemporaries often give women characters central roles, with figures like Dilsey in *The Sound and the Fury* and Addie Bundren in *As I Lay Dying*, but never grant them an independent voice. The mediating, reflective narrator is consistently male. Even in *As I Lay Dying*, Addie is granted only one chapter while her sons occupy the majority of the narrative.

5. For a discussion of southern honor and the chivalric code, see Wyatt-Brown and Watson, especially chapters 1 and 2.

6. Later, Scarlett's wish for an expensive and garish house after her marriage to Rhett is an example of her desire to show off her wealth. When members of the aristocracy, now the genteel poor, refuse to recognize her socially, she realizes that no amount of money can buy her respectability.

7. An interesting comparison might be made here between Mitchell's representation of matrilineage and Alice Walker's. See Walker's

essay "In Search of Our Mothers' Gardens" in the collection by the same name (231–43). Walker stresses the "inheritance" of creativity and story while Mitchell's novel emphasizes endurance and an ability to break social codes.

8. Although Glasgow and Mitchell both champion the national myth of the yeoman farmer with their women protagonists Dorinda and Scarlett, Glasgow questions Dorinda's individual "vein of iron" with her later women characters. Ada Fincastle and Kate Oliver (*In This Our Life* [1941]) are female farmers who value community. Harriette Arnow's *The Dollmaker* also challenges the value of competitive individualism.

9. See Jackson for a discussion of the rise of the Klan during the 1920s, the period when Mitchell was writing *GWTW*. Fear of blacks and immigrants rose to alarming proportions in American cities during the postwar urban migration in the early 1920s (9–23).

Chapter 3

1. Stouck defines Cather's "pastoral mode" as an essentially nostalgic, psychological mood rather than merely the use of rural scenery (37). Rosowski (*The Voyage Perilous*) focuses on the celebratory pastoral mode represented by *O Pioneers!* Although Fryer refutes the misreading of Cather's pastoralism as a substitution of the male landscape myth, she too concentrates on the author's midwestern "soil novels" without considering the southern landscape (229–60). I see *Sapphira*, however, as a different kind of pastoral, in which Cather is more critical of southern society yet curiously less judgmental of individual characters.

2. Rosowski and Woodress place the novel in the gothic tradition. Woodress comments: "Cather used Virginia in the waning days of the slave system to provide the milieu for her contest between good and evil. The iniquities of slavery served well as a vehicle for her darkening vision" (484).

3. Stouck paraphrases a letter Cather wrote to Dorothy Canfield Fisher on October 14, 1940 (226).

4. It is important to note here that although Cather rejects one

damaging stereotype of the black woman—that as seductress—she succumbs to another when she describes "the foolish, dreamy, nigger side of [Nancy's] nature" (178). Cather's ability to recognize Nancy's victimization here is thus *more* remarkable in light of her more "typical" view of black "nature."

5. This is one of Cather's later stories, published in *Obscure Destinies* (1932) along with two other "western" stories, "Neighbour Rosicky" and "Two Friends." Although the story takes place in Colorado, the tone of the story resembles *Sapphira* more in its concern for manners and form as well as the underlying victimization of women.

6. Bailey paraphrases: "A pioneer, should, in other words, be capable of ignoring a traditional social order in favour of a not yet realized re-vision and a re-ordered way of life" (397).

Chapter 4

1. See, for instance, Elizabeth Madox Roberts's *The Time of Man* (1926) and Edith Summers Kelley's *Weeds* (1922). In both novels, the young heroine's appreciation of nature and love of farming is precluded by the role of childbearing.

2. Compare this scene with Nathan's heroism at the train wreck in *Barren Ground*. Courageous acts of mothers often go unrecognized because they occur outside the public realm.

3. See Murfree's *In the Tennessee Mountains* (1884), for instance.

4. Schafer maintains that "Arnow opened the scope of her narrative by contrasting two kinds of proletarian worlds: a world of 'rural virtues,' of some pastoral charm . . . versus a world of factories, polluted air, concrete, and machine work" (48–49). By depicting the transference of the poor white working class from the farm to the factory, however, Arnow not only emphasizes the dehumaniz-ing effect of this migration but reveals the growing difficulty for rural inhabitants to make a living off their land. See Cratis Williams (388).

5. Arnow insists in a letter responding to an article on *The Dollmaker* by Barbara Rigney, that capitalism is not solely a result of industrial

society but an outgrowth of the individualistic rural values of property ownership and productivity. She writes: ". . . wasn't Gertie when in the hills something of a capitalist: she sold every egg she could spare, and was saving money for the purpose of buying a farm of her own . . ." ("Letter to Barbara Rigney"). While the novel does not reject patriarchal or capitalistic values directly, it does, I contend, begin to imagine alternative communal values to counteract economic individualism. The women at Merry Hill bridge both class and cultural barriers in order to provide for and protect their families.

6. See the Introduction for more discussion of the nature of women's communities in female pastoral. Goodman also discusses the formation of a community of women in the novel in "The Multi-Ethnic Community of Women in Harriette Arnow's *The Dollmaker*."

7. Unlike Celie in *The Color Purple*, Gertie cannot sustain the creativity she draws from nature—Celie is separated from her biological children early on and is thus able to develop an independent, artistic identity. Edwards discusses Gertie's developing artistry in her chapter, "Makers of Art, Makers of Life: Creativity and Community in *Sula, Their Eyes Were Watching God*, and *The Dollmaker*" (188–235).

8. In discussing the difficulty of Arnow's mother-artistry, Hobbs sees the novel itself as the author's "Callie Lou" ("A Portrait of the Artist" 866).

9. Hobbs quotes Strauss's letter to Arnow October 24, 1935 ("Starting Out" 147). This correspondence is contained in the University of Kentucky Library's Special Collections on Arnow.

10. This story was edited by Glenda Hobbs and published for the first time in *The Georgia Review* 33 (Winter 1979): 867–75.

Chapter 5

1. Among the critics who hold this view are Bernard Bell and Robert Stepto. Some black feminist critics, like Hazel Carby and Jean Fagan Yellin argue with the use of the slave narrative as the

primary model of African-American literature since most of the extant narratives were composed by men. See Yellin's introduction to Jacobs (xxv–xxxiv).

2. The critical acclaim this novel received suggests that the academy also viewed the South as an inappropriate locus for black fiction. White critics consistently point to the "Harlem Renaissance" as the flowering of African-American fiction, ignoring other contemporary black southern authors. See, for instance, King (1980), who claims: "Their great theme was the attempt (literally) to escape the white South which had historically oppressed their people" (8).

3. Trudier Harris denounces this visionary format of Walker's fiction in a recent article: "The re-entry into Southern territory in *The Color Purple* and the conquering of restriction placed on black women in that territory makes the novel a new breed of fairy tale. Meridian may be a legend, but Celie is an ugly duckling turned princess" (6)—which, of course, is precisely my point. The female pastoral *is* a visionary genre.

4. While the parallels between Celie's experience and slavery are clear, I do not want to place the novel in the context of slave narrative. Celie is oppressed both by Albert and by the society in which she lives, but her growth to selfhood and claiming of a voice is only metaphorically "escape" from bondage. In the next chapter, Sherley Williams's protagonist Dessa must escape both physically and psychologically from slavery, and Williams's novel borrows more directly from slave narrative conventions. For more on *The Color Purple's* resemblance to this genre, see Hernton and Tucker.

5. See also Walker's essay, "In Search of Our Mothers' Gardens" (231–43). Walker defines black women's creativity using the metaphor of the garden and describes her mother's artistry: "I notice that it is only when my mother is working in her flowers that she is radiant, almost to the point of being invisible—except as Creator, hand and eye. She is involved in work her soul must have. Ordering the universe in the image of her personal conception of beauty" (241).

6. Henry Louis Gates, Jr., has examined how African-American writers "signify" upon one another's texts as well as parodying earlier

literary forms by white authors. He explains how *Their Eyes* revised not only Toomer's *Cane* but also DuBois's *Quest* and Douglass's *Narrative* ("The blackness of blackness" 290).

7. On this point see McDowell's introduction to *Quicksand* (xvi).

Chapter 6

1. See Chesnutt's *The Colonel's Dream* (1905) and his short story collections *The Conjure Woman* (1899) and *The Wife of his Youth* (1899). Arna Bontemps is one of the few black writers to use an antebellum setting in *Black Thunder* (1936), his historical novel about a slave revolt.

2. See Spillers for an explanation of why chronological comparisons of black women writers are not always appropriate. Her discussion of the differences between Toni Morrison's *Sula* and Margaret Walker's *Jubilee* is relevant to *Dessa Rose*. While *Jubilee* and *Dessa Rose* both recast the antebellum South, the earlier novel, Spillers observes, conforms to a more heroic or one-dimensional narrative form: "From this angle of advocacy and preservation the writer does not penetrate the core of experience, but encircles it" (187). In this sense, although the subject is quite different, *Dessa* has more in common with *Sula* than *Jubilee* since Williams and Morrison are more concerned with characters' consciousness. Also, Morrison's most recent novel, *Beloved* (1987), as well as Gloria Naylor's *Mama Day* (1988), follows both Williams's multidimensional form and her subject.

3. See Olney for a list of and commentary on these conventions (152–54). He has made an extensive, Proppian analysis of the slave narrative genre.

4. See Yellin, "Text and Contexts of Harriet Jacob's *Incidents in the Life of a Slave Girl: Written by Herself,*" in Davis and Gates 262–82 and her introduction to Jacobs (xiii–xxxiv).

5. I am indebted to McDowell's analysis of the various namings and renamings of Dessa's experience in the novel. Her thesis is as follows: "*Dessa Rose* stages multiple and often contradictory versions of Dessa's enslavement and subsequent versions that

underscore well-rehearsed and commonplace assumptions about the difficulty . . . of ascertaining the 'Truth.' And yet the novel resists the pull of the postmodern orthodoxy of undecidability and relativism" ("Negotiating Between Tenses" 145).

6.   Doris Davenport remarks that Rufel "is full of contradictions and, like Scarlett O'Hara, puts off thinking not just until another day, but almost forever" (338). I believe this is not a valid comparison, for Rufel, unlike Scarlett, confronts her own ignorance about slavery and learns not only to stop her own exploitation but to reject the patriarchal system completely.

7.   See Carby (*Reconstructing Womanhood*) for an explanation of how the "mammy" in plantation literature represents the ultimate exploitation of the black female body (20–39).

8.   Lillian Smith explicates a "race-sex-sin spiral" which ultimately led to the lynching of black men: "The more trails the white man made to back-yard cabins, the higher he raised his white wife on her pedestal when he returned to the big house. . . . Then a time came . . . when man's suspicion of white woman began to pull the spiral higher and higher. It was of course inevitable for him to suspect her of the sins he had committed so pleasantly and often. *What if*. . . . Too often white woman could only smile bleakly in reply to the unasked question. But white man mistook this empty smile for one of cryptic satisfaction and in jealous panic began to project his own sins on to the Negro male" (116–17).

9.   Like the nature imagery in *The Color Purple*, this scene "signifies" upon Zora Neale Hurston's *Their Eyes Were Watching God*; Janie's Nanny tells her that black women are the mules of the world, and the mule becomes a trope for the suffering they must endure.

10. This scene recalls Cather's reunion of Till, Nancy, and Rachel at the end of *Sapphira and the Slave Girl*, only with an important revision. In Williams's novel the three women, two black and one white, unite to confront the power of patriarchy directly, unlike in the earlier pastoral where such authority must be subverted instead of challenged.

11. Fox-Genovese observes: "The privileged roles and identities of slaveholding women depended upon the oppression of slave

women, and the slave women knew it. Slaveholding and slave
women shared a world of mutual antagonism and frayed tempers
that frequently erupted in violence, cruelty, and even murder.
They also shared a world of physical and emotional intimacy that
is uncommon among women of antagonistic classes and different
races. Slaveholding women were elitist and racist. . . . [I]n some
essential respects, they were more crudely racist than their men"
(*Within the Plantation Household* 35). And Jacqueline Jones comes to
a similar conclusion: ". . . the denigration of white women, whether
manifested through physical force or in a more subtle, though no
less painful way, was part and parcel of slavery. By directing their
anger toward slave women, white wives achieved a fleeting moment
of catharsis. Rarely in American history is there a more striking
example of the way in which the patriarchal imperative could turn
woman against woman, white against black" (27).

Works Cited

Arnold, Marilyn. "Of Human Bondage: Cather's Subnarrative in *Sapphira and the Slave Girl." Mississippi Quarterly* 40 (Summer 1987): 323–88.

Arnow, Harriette Simpson. *The Dollmaker.* 1954. New York: Avon, 1972.

———. "Fra Lippi and Me." *Georgia Review* 33 (Winter 1979): 867–75.

———. *Hunter's Horn.* 1949. New York: Avon, 1979.

———. "Letter to Barbara Rigney." *Frontiers: A Journal of Women's Studies* 1:2 (1976): 147.

———. *Mountain Path.* New York: Covici-Friede, 1936.

———. *The Weedkiller's Daughter.* New York: Knopf, 1970.

Auerbach, Nina. *Communities of Women: An Idea in Fiction.* Cambridge, MA: Harvard UP, 1978.

Bailey, Jennifer. "The Dangers of Femininity in Willa Cather's Fiction." *Journal of American Studies* 16, no. 3 (Dec. 1982): 391–406.

Bargainner, Earl. "The Myth of Moonlight and Magnolias." *Louisiana Studies* 15 (Spring 1976): 5–20.

Bartley, Numan, ed. *The Evolution of Southern Culture.* Athens: U of Georgia P, 1988.

Baym, Nina. "Melodramas of Beset Manhood: How Theories of American Fiction Exclude Women Authors." *American Quarterly* 33 (1981). Rpt. in *The New Feminist Criticism: Essays on Women, Literature, and Theory.* Ed. Elaine Showalter. New York: Pantheon, 1985. 63–80.

Bell, Bernard. *The Afro-American Novel and Its Tradition.* Amherst: U of Massachusetts P, 1987.

Bellah, Robert N., et al. *Habits of the Heart: Individualism and Commitment in American Life.* Berkeley: U of California P, 1985.

Bleikasten, André. "In Praise of Helen." *Faulkner and Women: Faulkner and Yoknapatawpha, 1985.* Eds. Doreen Fowler and Ann Abadie. Jackson: UP of Mississippi, 1986. 128–43.

Bloom, Harold, ed. *William Faulkner's Light in August: Modern Critical Interpretations.* New York: Chelsea, 1988.

Bond, Tonette L. "Pastoral Transformations in *Barren Ground.*" *Mississippi Quarterly* 32 (Fall 1979): 565–76.

Bone, Robert. *Down Home: Origins of the Afro-American Short Story.* New York: Columbia UP, 1975.

Bontemps, Arna. *Black Thunder.* 1936. Boston: Beacon Press, 1968.

Bradbury, John M. *Renaissance in the South: A Critical History of the Literature, 1920–1960.* Chapel Hill: U of North Carolina P, 1963.

Brown, E. K. *Willa Cather: A Critical Biography.* New York: Knopf, 1953.

Buck, Paul H. *The Road to Reunion: 1865–1900.* Boston: Little, Brown, 1937.

Burke, Fielding. *Call Home the Heart.* 1932. Old Westbury, CT: Feminist Press, 1983.

Caldwell, Erskine. *Tobacco Road.* 1932. Rpt. New York: Modern Library, 1947.

Carby, Hazel V. "Ideologies of Black Folk: The Historical Novel of Slavery." McDowell and Rampersad 125–43.

———. "'On the Threshold of Woman's Era': Lynching, Empire, and Sexuality in Black Feminist Theory." *Critical Inquiry* 12 (Autumn 1985): 262–77.

———. *Reconstructing Womanhood: The Emergence of the Afro-American Woman Novelist.* New York: Oxford UP, 1987.

Carlin, Deborah. "Enslaved by History: The Burden of the Past and Cather's Last Novel." Paper read at MLA Convention. New Orleans, 29 Dec. 1988.

Cash, W. J. *The Mind of the South.* New York: Knopf, 1941.

Castiglia, Chris. Diss. Columbia U, 1989.

Cather, Willa. *A Lost Lady.* 1923. Rpt. New York: Knopf, 1945.

———. *My Antonia.* 1918. Rpt. Boston: Houghton-Mifflin, 1946.

———. *Obscure Destinies.* 1930. Rpt. New York: Knopf, 1932.

———. *O Pioneers!* 1913. Rpt. Boston: Houghton-Mifflin, 1936.

———. *Sapphira and the Slave Girl.* 1940. Rpt. New York: Vintage, 1975.

———. *The Song of the Lark.* 1915. Rpt. Boston: Houghton-Mifflin, 1943.

Chase, Richard. *The American Novel and Its Tradition.* Garden City: Doubleday, 1957.

Chesnutt, Charles. *The Colonel's Dream.* 1905. Rpt. Negro University Press, 1970.

——. *The Conjure Woman.* 1899. Ann Arbor: U of Michigan P, 1969.

Chopin, Kate. *The Awakening.* 1899. Rpt. New York: Norton, 1976.

Christian, Barbara. "Alice Walker: The Black Woman Artist as Wayward." *Black Women Writers (1950–1980): A Critical Evaluation.* Ed. Mari Evans. Garden City: Doubleday, 1984. 458–77.

——. "Somebody Forgot to Tell Somebody Something: The Historical Novels of Contemporary Afro-American Women." The Scholar and the Feminist XV Conference, Barnard College, New York City, Mar. 26, 1988.

Cohn, Jan. *Romance and the Erotics of Property.* Durham: Duke UP, 1988.

Conkin, Paul. "The South in Southern Agrarianism." Bartley 131–45.

Cook, Sylvia Jenkins. *From Tobacco Road to Route 66: The Southern Poor White in Fiction.* Chapel Hill: U of North Carolina P, 1976.

Davenport, Doris. Review of *Dessa Rose. Black American Literature Forum* 20 (Fall 1986): 335–40.

Davis, Charles T., and Henry Louis Gates, Jr. eds. *The Slave's Narrative.* Oxford: Oxford UP, 1985.

Davis, Thadious M. "Some Standard-Bearers in the New Negro Renaissance." Rubin et al. 291–313.

Dixon, Melvin. *Ride Out the Wilderness: Geography and Identity in Afro-American Literature.* Urbana : U of Illinois P, 1987.

Du Plessis, Rachel Blau. *Writing Beyond the Ending: Narrative Strategies of Twentieth Century Women Writers.* Bloomington: Indiana UP, 1985.

Edwards, Anne. *The Road to Tara: The Life of Margaret Mitchell.* New Haven, CT: Tucker and Fields, 1983.

Edwards, Lee. *Psyche as Hero: Female Heroism and Fictional Form.* Middletown, CT: Wesleyan UP, 1984.

Ellison, Ralph. *Invisible Man.* New York: Random House, 1952.

Empson, William. *Some Versions of Pastoral.* 1935. Rpt. New York: New Directions, 1960.

Faulkner, William. *The Hamlet.* 1940. Rpt. New York: Random House, 1964.

——. *Light in August.* 1932. Rpt. New York: Random House, 1959.

——. *The Sound and the Fury.* 1929. Rpt. New York: Modern Library, 1956.

———. "That Evening Sun." *Collected Stories of William Faulkner*. New York: Random House, 1950.

———. *The Unvanquished*. 1934. Rpt. New York: Random House, 1965.

Fauset, Jessie. *Plum Bun: A Novel Without a Moral*. 1928. Rpt. London: Pandora Press, 1985.

Ferber, Edna. *So Big*. New York: Grosset and Dunlap, 1924.

Fiedler, Leslie. "*Gone with the Wind*: The Feminization of the Anti-Tom Novel." *What Was Literature? Class Culture and Mass Society*. New York: Simon and Schuster, 1982. 197–212.

———. *The Return of the Vanishing American*. New York: Stein and Day, 1968.

Fox-Genovese, Elizabeth. "Scarlett O'Hara: the Southern Lady as New Woman." *American Quarterly* 33 (Fall 1981): 391–411.

———. *Within the Plantation Household: Black and White Women of the Old South*. Chapel Hill: U of North Carolina P, 1988.

Fryer, Judith. *Felicitous Space: The Imaginative Structures of Edith Wharton and Willa Cather*. Chapel Hill: U of North Carolina P, 1986.

Ganim, Carole. "Herself: Women and Place in Appalachian Literature." *Appalachian Journal* 13 (Spring 1986): 258–74.

Gates, Henry Louis, Jr. "The blackness of blackness: a critique of the sign and the Signifying Monkey." *Critical Inquiry* 9, no. 4 (1983). Rpt. in *Black Literature and Literary Theory*. Ed. Henry Louis Gates, Jr. New York: Methuen, 1984. 285–321.

Gelfant, Blanche. "*Gone with the Wind* and the Impossibilities of Fiction." *Women Writing in America: Voices in Collage*. Hanover: UP of New England, 1984.

Genovese, Eugene D. *Roll Jordan Roll: The World the Slaves Made*. New York: Pantheon, 1974.

Gilbert, Sandra M., and Susan Gubar. *The Madwoman in the Attic: The Woman Writer and the Nineteenth Century Literary Imagination*. New Haven: Yale UP, 1979.

———. *No Man's Land: The Place of the Woman Writer in the Twentieth Century*. Vol. 1 *The War of the Words*. New Haven: Yale UP, 1988.

Glasgow, Ellen. *Barren Ground*. 1925. Rpt. San Diego: Harcourt, 1985.

———. *The Battle-Ground*. 1902. Rpt. Garden City, NY: Doubleday, 1937.

———. *Beyond Defeat: An Epilogue to an Era*. Ed. with an introduction by Luther Y. Gore. Charlottesville: UP of Virginia, 1966.

———. *A Certain Measure: An Interpretation of Prose Fiction.* New York: Harcourt, 1943.

———. *The Collected Stories of Ellen Glasgow.* Ed. Richard K. Meeker. Baton Rouge: Louisiana State UP, 1963.

———. *The Deliverance.* New York: Doubleday, 1904.

———. *Ellen Glasgow's Reasonable Doubts: A Collection of Her Writings.* Ed. Julius Rowan Raper. Baton Rouge: Louisiana State UP, 1988.

———. *In This Our Life.* New York: Harcourt, 1941.

———. *Life and Gabriella.* Garden City, NY: Doubleday, 1916.

———. *The Miller of Old Church.* Garden City: Doubleday, 1911.

———. *Vein of Iron.* 1925. Rpt. San Diego: Harcourt, 1983.

———. *Virginia.* New York: Doubleday, 1913.

Goldstein, Laurence. "The Image of Detroit in Twentieth Century Literature." *Michigan Quarterly Review* 25 (Spring 1986): 269–91.

Goodman, Charlotte. "The Multi-Ethnic Community of Women in Harriette Arnow's *The Dollmaker.*" *MELUS* 10 (Winter 1983): 49–53.

Gray, Richard. *The Literature of Memory: Modern Writers of the American South.* Baltimore: Johns Hopkins UP, 1977.

———. *Writing the South: Ideas of an American Region.* New York: Cambridge UP, 1986.

Gwin, Minrose C. *Black and White Women of the Old South: The Peculiar Sisterhood in American Literature.* Knoxville: U of Tennessee P, 1985.

Hamner, Eugénie Lambert. "The unknown, well-known child in Cather's last novel. *Women's Studies* 11 (1984): 346–57.

Hardy, John Edward. "Ellen Glasgow." *Southern Renascence: The Literature of the Modern South.* Eds. Louis D. Rubin, Jr., and Robert D. Jacobs. Baltimore: Johns Hopkins UP, 1953. 236–50.

Harper, Francis. *Iola Leroy or Shadows Uplifted.* 1893. Introduction by Frances Smith Foster. Rpt. New York: Oxford, 1988.

Harris, Trudier. "From Victimization to Free Enterprise: Alice Walker's *The Color Purple.*" *Studies in American Fiction* 14 (Spring 1986): 1–17.

Harwell, Richard, ed. *Margaret Mitchell's* Gone with the Wind *Letters.* New York: Macmillan, 1976.

Heilbrun, Carolyn G. "What Was Penelope Unweaving." *Hamlet's Mother and Other Women.* New York: Columbia UP, 1990. 103–11.

Hernton, Calvin C. "Who's Afraid of Alice Walker?" *The Sexual Mountain*

and Black Women Writers: Adventures in Sex, Literature and Real Life.
New York: Doubleday, 1987. 1–36.

Hite, Molly. "Writing—and Reading—the Body: Female Sexuality and
Recent Feminist Fiction." *Feminist Studies* 14 (Spring 1988): 121–42.

Hobbs, Glenda. "A Portrait of the Artist as Mother: Harriette Arnow and
The Dollmaker." *Georgia Review* 33 (Winter 1979): 851–66.

———. "Starting Out in the Thirties: Harriette Arnow's Literary
Genesis." *Literature at the Barricades: The American Writer in the 1930s.*
Eds. Ralph Bogardus and Fred Hobson. University, AL: U of
Alabama P, 1982. 144–61.

Hopkins, Pauline. *Contending Forces.* 1899. Rpt. New York: Oxford UP,
1988.

Hurston, Zora Neale. *Their Eyes Were Watching God.* 1937. Rpt. Urbana: U
of Illinois P, 1978.

Irvin, Helen. "Gea in Georgia: A Mythic Dimension in *Gone with the
Wind.*" Pyron, *Recasting* Gone with the Wind *in American Culture* 57–
68.

Jackson, Kenneth. *The Ku Klux Klan in the City: 1915–1930.* New York:
Oxford, 1967.

Jacobs, Harriet A. *Incidents in the Life of a Slave Girl.* 1861. Ed. with an
introduction by Jean Fagan Yellin. Cambridge: Harvard UP, 1987.

Jones, Anne Goodwyn. "*Gone with the Wind* and Others: Popular Fiction,
1920–1950." Rubin, *The History of Southern Literature* 363–74.

———. *Tomorrow Is Another Day: The Woman Writer in the South, 1859–1936.*
Baton Rouge: Louisiana State UP, 1981.

Jones, Jacqueline. *Labor of Love, Labor of Sorrow: Black Women, Work, and the
Family from Slavery to the Present.* New York: Basic Books, 1985.

Kaplan, Cora. "History as Prophecy: *Dessa Rose* and *Beloved.*" Paper read at
MLA Convention, New Orleans, Dec. 1989.

Kelley, Edith Summers. *Weeds.* 1923. Rpt. New York: The Feminist Press,
1982.

Kennedy, John Pendleton. *Swallow Barn* or *A Sojourn in the Old Dominion.*
1832. Rpt. Baton Rouge: Louisiana State UP, 1986.

King, Richard H. "The 'Simple Story's' Ideology: *Gone with the Wind* and
the New South Creed." Pyron, *Recasting* Gone with the Wind *in
American Culture* 167–83.

———. *A Southern Renaissance: The Cultural Awakening of the American South: 1930–1955*. New York: Oxford UP, 1980.

Kitch, Sally L. "Gender and language: dialect, silence and the disruption of discourse." *Women's Studies* 14 (1987): 65–78.

Kolodny, Annette. *The Land Before Her: Fantasy and Experience of the American Frontiers, 1630–1860*. Chapel Hill: U of North Carolina P, 1984.

———. *The Lay of the Land: Metaphor as Experience and History in American Life and Letters*. Chapel Hill: U of North Carolina P, 1975.

Kreyling, Michael. *Figures of the Hero in Southern Narrative*. Baton Rouge: Louisiana State UP, 1986.

Larsen, Nella. *Quicksand* and *Passing*. 1928, 1929. Ed. with an introduction by Deborah McDowell. New Brunswick, NJ: Rutgers UP, 1986.

Lee, Dorothy. "Harriette Arnow's *Dollmaker*: A Journey to Awareness." *Critique* 20, no. 2 (1978): 92–98.

Lentz, Perry Carlton. "Our Missing Epic: A Study in the Novels about the American Civil War." Diss. Vanderbilt U, 1970.

Lewis, Edith. *Willa Cather Living: A Personal Record*. New York: Knopf, 1953.

MacKethan, Lucinda. *The Dream of Arcady: Place and Time in Southern Literature*. Baton Rouge: Louisiana State UP, 1980.

———. "Plantation Fiction, 1865–1900." Rubin et al. 209–18.

Malpezzi, Francis M. "Silence and Captivity in Babylon: Harriette Arnow's *The Dollmaker*." *Southern Studies* 20 (Spring 1981): 84–90.

Marx, Leo. *The Machine in the Garden*. New York: Oxford UP, 1964.

Mason, Bobbie Ann. *Shiloh and other stories*. New York: Harper and Row, 1982.

May, Robert, "*Gone with the Wind* as Southern History: A Reappraisal." *Southern Quarterly* 17 (Fall 1978–79): 51–64.

McDowell, Deborah. "'The Changing Same'": Generational Connections and Black Women Novelists." *New Literary History* 18 (Winter 1987): 281–302.

———. "Negotiating Between Tenses: Witnessing Slavery After Freedom—*Dessa Rose*." McDowell and Rampersad 144–63.

———, and Arnold Rampersad, eds. *Slavery and the Literary Imagination*. Selected Papers from the English Institute. New Series, 13. Baltimore: Johns Hopkins UP, 1987.

Miller, Danny. "A MELUS Interview: Harriette Arnow." *MELUS* 9 (Summer 1982): 83–97.

Mitchell, Margaret. *Gone with the Wind.* 1936. Rpt. New York: Avon, 1973.

Mixon, Wayne. "Humor, Romance, and Realism at the Turn of the Century." Rubin et al. 246–51.

Moers, Ellen. *Literary Women: The Great Writers.* New York: Doubleday, 1976.

Mootry, Maria Katella. *Studies in Black Pastoral: Five Afro-American Writers.* Diss. Northwestern U, 1974.

Morrison, Toni. *The Bluest Eye.* London: Chatto and Windus, 1979.

Murfree, Mary Noailles. *In the Tennessee Mountains.* 1884. Ridgewood, NJ: Gregg Press, 1968.

Murr, Judy Smith. "History in *Barren Ground* and *Vein of Iron*: Theory, Structure, and Symbol." *The Southern Literary Journal* 8 (Fall 1975): 39–54.

Naylor, Gloria. *Mama Day.* New York: Ticknor and Fields, 1988.

Newman, Francis. *The Hard-Boiled Virgin.* 1926. Rpt. Athens: U of Georgia P, 1980.

O'Brien, Sharon. *Willa Cather: The Emerging Voice.* New York: Oxford UP, 1987.

Olney, James. "'I Was Born': Slave Narratives, Their Status as Autobiography and as Literature." Davis and Gates 148–74.

Page, Thomas Nelson. *In Ole Virginia.* 1887. Rpt. Chapel Hill: The U of North Carolina P, 1969.

Painter, Nell Irvin. "'Social Equality,' Miscegenation, Labor, and Power." Bartley 47–67.

Parker-Smith, Bettye J. "Alice Walker's Women: In Search of Some Peace of Mind." *Black Women Writers (1950–1980): A Critical Evaluation.* Ed. Mari Evans. Garden City, NY: Anchor, 1984. 478–93.

Payne, Ladell. "Ellen Glasgow's *Vein of Iron*: Vanity, Irony, Idiocy." *The Mississippi Quarterly* 31 (Winter 1977–78): 57–66.

Porter, Katherine Anne. *Flowering Judas.* 1930. Rpt. New York: Random House, 1956.

Pyron, Darden. "The Inner War of Southern History." Pyron, *Recasting Gone with the Wind in American Culture* 185–201.

———, ed. *Recasting Gone with the Wind in American Culture.* Miami: UP of Florida, 1983.

Raper, Julius Rowan. *From the Sunken Garden: The Fiction of Ellen Glasgow, 1916–1945.* Baton Rouge: Louisiana State UP, 1980.

———. *Without Shelter: The Early Career of Ellen Glasgow.* Baton Rouge: Louisiana State UP, 1971.

Ridgely, J. V. *Nineteenth Century Southern Literature.* Lexington: UP of Kentucky, 1980.

Roberts, Elizabeth Madox. *The Great Meadow.* New York: Viking, 1930.

———. *The Time of Man.* New York: Viking, 1926.

Robinson, Phyllis C. *Willa: The Life of Willa Cather.* Garden City, NY: Doubleday, 1983.

Rölvaag, Ole. *Giants in the Earth.* 1927. New York: Harper, 1929.

Rosowski, Susan J. *The Voyage Perilous: Willa Cather's Romanticism.* Lincoln: U of Nebraska P, 1986.

———. "Willa Cather's American Gothic: *Sapphira and the Slave Girl.*" *Great Plains Quarterly* 4 (Fall 1984): 220–30.

Rubin, Louis D., Jr. "Scarlett O'Hara and the Two Quentin Compsons." *A Gallery of Southerners.* Baton Rouge: Louisiana State UP, 1982. 26–48.

———, et al., eds. *The History of Southern Literature.* Baton Rouge: Louisiana State UP, 1985.

Schafer, William J. "Carving Out a Life: *The Dollmaker* Revisited." *Appalachian Journal* 14 (Winter 1986): 46–50.

Schmidt, Jan Zlotnik. "Ellen Glasgow's Heroic Legends: A Study of *Life and Gabriella, Barren Ground,* and *Vein of Iron.*" *Tennessee Studies in Literature.* Eds. Allison Ensor and Thomas Heffernan. Vol. 26. Knoxville: U of Tennessee P, 1981. 117–41.

Schultz, Elizabeth. "Out of the Woods and into the World: A Study of Interracial Friendships between Women in American Novels." *Conjuring: Black Women, Fiction, and Literary Tradition.* Eds. Marjorie Pryse and Hortense J. Spillers. Bloomington: Indiana UP, 1985. 67–85.

Scott, Anne Firor. *The Southern Lady: from pedestal to politics, 1830–1930.* Chicago: U of Chicago P, 1970.

Seidel, Kathryn Lee. *The Southern Belle in the American Novel.* Tampa: U of South Florida P, 1985.

Shelby, Anne. "Harriette Arnow: 'The Alley' and the Promised Land." *Appalachian Heritage* 14 (Winter 1986): 48–50.

Shelton, Frank W. "Alienation and Integration in Alice Walker's *The Color Purple.*" *College Language Association Journal* 28 (June 1985): 382–92.

Showalter, Elaine, ed. *The New Feminist Criticism: Essays on Women, Literature, and Theory.* New York: Pantheon, 1985.

Simms, William Gilmore. *The Yemassee.* 1835. Rpt. New York: A. C. Armstrong and Sons, 1882.

Simpson, Lewis P. *The Dispossessed Garden: Pastoral and History in Southern Literature.* Athens: U of Georgia P, 1975.

Singal, Donald J. *The War Within: From Victorian to Modernist Thought in the South, 1919–1945.* Chapel Hill: U of North Carolina P, 1982.

Skaggs, Merrill Maguire. "Willa Cather's Experimental Southern Novel." *The Mississippi Quarterly* 35 (Winter 1981–82): 3–14.

Slotkin, Richard. *Regeneration through Violence: The Mythology of the American Frontier, 1600–1860.* Middletown, CT: Wesleyan UP, 1973.

Smith, Henry Nash. *Virgin Land: The American West as Symbol and Myth.* Cambridge: Harvard UP, 1950.

Smith, Lee. *Oral History.* New York: Ballantine, 1983.

Smith, Lillian. *Killers of the Dream.* New York: Norton, 1961.

Spillers, Hortense J. "A Hateful Passion, A Lost Love." *Feminist Issues in Literary Scholarship.* Ed. Shari Benstock. Bloomington: Indiana UP, 1987. 181–207.

Steinem, Gloria. "Alice Walker: Do You Know This Woman? She Knows You." *Outrageous Acts and Everyday Rebellions.* New York: Holt, 1983. 259–75.

Stepto, Robert. *From Behind the Veil: A Study of Afro-American Narrative.* Urbana: U of Illinois P, 1979.

Stouck, David. *Willa Cather's Imagination.* Lincoln: U of Nebraska P, 1975.

Tate, Allen. *The Fathers.* 1938. Rpt. Baton Rouge: Louisiana State UP, 1977.

Tate, Claudia, ed. *Black Women Writers at Work.* New York: Continuum, 1983.

Taylor, Helen. "*Gone with the Wind*: The Mammy of Them All." *The Progress of Romance: The Politics of Popular Fiction.* Ed. Jean Radford. London: Routledge & Kegan Paul, 1986. 113–36.

Thiébaux, Marcelle. *Ellen Glasgow.* New York: Ungar, 1982.

Toomer, Jean. *Cane.* 1923. New York: University Place Press, 1967.

Tucker, Lindsey. "Alice Walker's *The Color Purple*: Emergent Woman, Emergent Text." *Black American Literature Forum* 22 (Spring 1988): 81–95.

Wagner, Linda Welshimer. *Ellen Glasgow: Beyond Convention*. Austin: U of Texas P, 1982.

Walker, Alice. *The Color Purple*. 1982. Rpt. New York: Pocket Books, 1985.

———. *In Search of Our Mothers' Gardens*. San Diego: Harcourt Brace Jovanovich, 1983.

———. *Meridian*. 1976. Rpt. New York: Pocket Books, 1988.

———. *The Temple of My Familiar*. San Diego: Harcourt Brace Jovanovich, 1989.

———. *The Third Life of Grange Copeland*. 1970. Rpt. New York: Pocket Books, 1988.

———. *You Can't Keep a Good Woman Down*. New York: Harcourt, 1981.

Walker, Margaret. *Jubilee*. Boston: Houghton-Mifflin, 1966.

Walker, Nancy. "Women Writers and Literary Naturalism: The Case of Ellen Glasgow." *American Literary Realism* 18 (Spring–Summer 1985): 133–46.

Walsh, Kathleen. "*Hunter's Horn*: Harriette Arnow's Subversive Hunting Tale." *Southern Literary Journal* 17 (Fall 1984): 54–67.

Warren, Robert Penn. *Meet Me in the Green Glen*. New York: Random House, 1971.

Watkins, Floyd. "*Gone with the Wind* as Vulgar Literature." *Southern Literary Journal* 2 (Spring 1970): 86–103.

Watson, Ritchie Devon. *The Cavalier in Virginia Fiction*. Baton Rouge: Louisiana State UP, 1985.

Weissman, Judith. *Half Savage and Hardy and Free: Women and Rural Radicalism in the Nineteenth-Century Novel*. Middletown, CT: Wesleyan UP, 1987.

Westling, Louise. *Sacred Groves and Ravaged Gardens: The Fiction of Eudora Welty, Carson McCullers, and Flannery O'Connor*. Athens: U of Georgia P, 1985.

Wharton, Edith. *Summer*. New York: D. Appelton and Co., 1917.

Williams, Cratis. "The Southern Mountaineer in Fact and Fiction Parts II–IV." *Appalachian Journal* 3 (Winter, Spring, Summer 1976): 134–392.

Williams, Raymond. *The Country and the City*. London: Chatto and Windus, 1973.

Williams, Sherley. *Dessa Rose*. 1986. New York: Berkley Books, 1987.

———. "Meditations on History." *Midnight Birds: stories by contemporary Black women writers*. Ed. Mary Helen Washington. Garden City, NY: Anchor, 1980. 200–248.

Williamson, Joel. "How Black was Rhett Butler?" Bartley 87–107.

Woodress, James. *Willa Cather: A Literary Life*. Lincoln: U of Nebraska P, 1987.

Woodward, C. Vann. *The Burden of Southern History*. New York: Vintage, 1960.

Wright, Richard. *Black Boy*. 1945. Cleveland: The World Publishing Co., 1947.

Wyatt-Brown, Bertram. "The Evolution of Heroes' Honor in the Southern Literary Tradition." Bartley 108–30.

Index

Female Pastoral was designed by Dariel Mayer and composed at the University of Tennessee Press on the Apple Macintosh. Linotronic camera pages were generated by AMPM, Inc. The book is set in New Baskerville and printed on 60-lb Glatfelter Natural. Manufactured in the United States of America by Cushing/Malloy, Inc.